BECOMING PREFERRED

How To Outsell Your Competition

by
Michael Vickers

SUMMIT
PRESS

Summit Press
A Division of Summit Learning Systems, Inc.
5445 DTC Parkway, Penthouse 4
Englewood, CO 80111

Visit our Web site at www.michaelvickers.com

This book may be purchased for business, educational, or sales promotional use. For information call: 800-367-5381

Production and Layout by Ryan Rayner
Edited by Austin Vickers
Copy Edited by Leslie Johnson
Printed and Bound in the United States of America
First Printing: January 2002
Second Printing
9 8 7 6 5 4 3 2 1
Library of Congress Cataloging-in-Publication Data

Vickers, Michael
Becoming Preferred: How to outsell your competition /
Michael Vickers.
p. cm.

ISBN - 0-971-3250-0-6

What Michael's Clients Say...

"Organizers like myself, place high value on presenters with practical experience who can deliver the message effectively. You delivered on both counts. Michael, always a pleasure to hear your pearls of wisdom."

Damian Borges, CAIFA

"We found Michael to be very professional, right on the mark with the topic we had chosen and very entertaining. For a group of bankers to make such glowing comments about a speaker who comes on right at the end of the day is saying something."

Sandy Duncan, Royal Bank Financial Group

"The information was top drawer and your presentation of it outstanding!"

Rhea Jorgensen, GE Capital

"I would like to take this opportunity to thank you for the presentation you made at our conference. Your contribution and subsequent formal and informal discussions lead to participants grading the conference "valuable and informative" and "the best ever"!"

Larry Stack, Neles Automation

"I certainly enjoyed your presentation at our sales congress. I have been using your closing strategy with great success."

Graham Calder, London Life

"Your energy and message is like a "shot in the arm". Students have told us that your presentation was informative, entertaining and a great way to wrap up our three day seminar. Other industry guest speakers scheduled to speak after you have also commented that they wish we would schedule you last, so that they do not have to follow your extraordinary presentation!"

David Maffitt, Phoenix Energy Marketing

"We have had very positive feedback from both the Management Team as well as our Financial Consultants who had the pleasure of hearing you speak. Many people walked out of the presentation with a new, positive outlook on their business and with new ideas to incorporate. We immediately saw ways to improve our business. In our own office, we have used your suggestions on numerous occasions already. You truly are an extraordinary speaker, living an extraordinary life!"

Esther Bast, Investors Group

"While I personally found the day to be educational as well as entertaining, the feedback that I have received from our employees who were at the session was completely positive. Your method of delivery ensured that participants were motivated throughout the day. It is indeed, information such as that which you delivered, which will keep CMHC competitive and carry us into the next millennium. Again Michael, thanks for a terrific event."

Don Renaud, CMHC

"You promised to have an impact and you were true to your promise. The feedback has been great and your insights into our business were very well received. They loved you!"

Paul Smith, Royal Bank

"You delivered a dynamic and insightful presentation that inspired, motivated and challenged everyone...By all reports, the conference was a success and your role as a keynote speaker contributed a great deal towards that result. Thank you again for delivering exactly what you promised – a presentation that would leave a lasting impression with the delegates. It was the perfect close for the conference!"

Marian Fox, CPSA

"The feedback we have received has been excellent – the conference participants really enjoyed your insights, energy and enthusiasm. Your contribution to the conference was very valuable – participants left the conference motivated and charged with energy."

Arlene Madell, Bank of Montreal

"You certainly motivated our troops! Your session was the most talked about after our conference."

Sarah Weilens, Syspro Software Ltd.

"Your presentation was outstanding and definitely fit the challenges and opportunities our newly merged organization faces...You truly were an inspiration to many in the audience and your comments caused many others to reflect on themselves and the way they conduct business. I know this will lead to success in our operations. It was the first time those 500 people were in a room together and you definitely were integral in getting our convention off to a great start."

Rob Moller, Mohawk - Husky

Contents

As the business landscape changes relentlessly, it is often a challenge to determine what our business strategy and primary focus should be. It seems that every month there is a new management or strategy fad that tempts us to change course and dramatically alter the way we do what we do in the world of commerce.

One thing is for certain: the environment within which enterprise will operate throughout the 21st Century will continue to be turbulent, uncertain and hyper-competitive. Companies that have enjoyed a competitive advantage based on their technological innovations will continue to see competitors bringing products and services to the market in real time.

The customer will have more choices than ever and, by virtue of the Internet, will be able to instantly compare your products and services against those of your competitor. The goal of today's business leader, entrepreneur or professional should be to become the preferred provider in the marketplace, that is, the one that customers run to in a crowded market because of the value you add and the way you treat them.

The three key strategies in "Becoming Preferred" proposed by Michael in this thoughtful and highly practical book represent a new philosophy for creating customer value while creating market differentiation.

Becoming Preferred, in my opinion, is a blueprint for all organizations who want to increase market share profitably and insulate their current customers from competitive erosion.

I am highly impressed with the simplicity yet effectiveness of Michael's message and the excellent way in which he illustrates his concepts with real life examples and tried and true business principles.

If you sell anything, this book will definitely help you become preferred.

Read it. Apply it. And then lead the field.

Robin Sharma, LL.M.
Bestselling Author of
"The Monk Who Sold His Ferrari"

Acknowledgements

It is with gratitude that I acknowledge some of the people who have helped me find my way in my career either through their encouragement or through their infinite wisdom.

Ross Gilchrist and Janet Alford who helped me define my message and style. Michael Smythe who taught me how to create Distinctive Value. To my friends and colleagues, too many to mention, you know who you are. My Gratitude.

Special thanks to my brother Austin who made sense of my ramblings and helped me communicate my thoughts in a meaningful way. Austin, you are a ten!

To my parents Hugh and Janet Vickers who have always supported and encouraged me.

Last but not least, the hundreds of companies that allowed me to integrate these concepts into their business process.

This work is dedicated to my children Ashley, Scott, Kendra and Lesley who are the joy of my life and to my life partner and best friend Beth.

Introduction

This book is divided into three sections, the first section focuses on differentiating yourself from the competition through Distinctive Value strategies. The second section focuses on re-engineering your sales process and the third section focuses on building the business relationship.

I have identified these three strategies as key elements to becoming preferred. For the past decade I have had the opportunity to implement these strategies with a number of my clients in a myriad of industries. I have seen them work with different variations, time and time again.

The secret to getting these strategies to work for you is execution. This is where most professionals and organizations drop the ball. They simply do not apply the strategies to their own process.

You will see very clearly within these pages that I suggest developing a well-defined process for creating Distinctive Value, managing the sales process and building the client relationship. These three areas cannot be left to chance. You must apply the process and be disciplined in your execution if you are to get them to work for you. You must take ownership of these strategies and tactics. You must refine them and make them work for you and you will enjoy all that comes from being preferred.

In today's competitive marketplace, the difference between top performing companies, mediocrity, and poverty is very little. While the difference is small, the consequences are often dramatic. In many cases, the difference can dictate whether or not your company survives and thrives, or whether it becomes an example in a business school text of how not to run a business. In every case, the difference will have a substantial impact on your company's performance.

Most of today's leading companies understand that you can improve performance by differentiating yourself through products and services. Thus, they spend millions of dollars in research and development doing just that. They also understand, however, that the end can never be achieved. In today's marketplace, it is difficult to create the ultimate product or service that does not require continuous innovation. Competitive advantage gained through the creation of new products and services is short lived and there is always a competitor willing and able to duplicate the offering. And soon.

So what is the answer to creating customer preference? Is there a key to creating a long-term competitive advantage? Is there a magic formula that will get you back into profitability? I believe there is. Not a magic bullet, but a formula that works like magic. A formula that I have seen time and time again move companies

"In order to succeed in today's highly competitive marketplace you must become the preferred provider of what you sell."

from the red into the black. A formula that has brought companies back into profitability that were on the brink of collapse. It is the same formula that significantly improves the performance of the sales professional. I have coached thousands of sales professionals throughout North America representing most business sectors. I have seen them double and triple their production by using this formula and the strategies and tactics outlined in this book.

In order to succeed in today's highly competitive marketplace you must become the *preferred* provider of what you sell. Preferred means that you, your company and your products are their first choice. It means that the market always comes to you first. Let me show you how to become preferred.

The Income Ladder

Picture a very tall ladder, at the top of which are sales professionals who earn millions of dollars each year. At the other end of the ladder are those who make the minimum wage. Question: Why are there sales people who will accept a minimum wage?

There could be dozens of reasons. Maybe it is their education, maybe it is their drive, maybe it is their experience, maybe they are content to not earn more. Regardless of the reason, and regardless of how much they make, the real question they should ask is: Do I make what I am worth? Am I where I should be on the income ladder? There are sales professionals at the $500,000 plus income level, there are sales professionals earning $250,000 a year, there are those making $100,000 a year and there are those making $50,000 or less. If you can think of an income level, there are sales professionals earning that kind of money. But again the big question. Are you currently being paid what you are worth?

This is the part where you might get angry with me. I suggest that you are being paid exactly what you are worth in the marketplace, as the market defines it. If not, why are you not earning more? I can show you how to change things if you would really like to increase your earning value.

You have two choices at this point: You can a) become a moaner and groaner and complain how you are a victim of the system and how badly life has treated you (in which case, I can probably do little for you), or b) you can take responsibility for your circumstances and admit that you are where you are because of your choices. If you choose option b and take responsibility for your position in life, I believe I can help you. Taking responsibility for your choices and present circumstances will empower you to make the necessary changes that will positively and significantly impact your income level.

So what is the key to moving up the income ladder? What is the secret to breaking your personal income ceiling and earning more than you ever have earned before? What is the difference between top performance, mediocrity, and poverty? I do not think it is a matter of working harder and putting in more time. Most sales professionals have about 2000 hours in their business year. You are probably no different. We all have the same amount of time to work with, so what is the difference? The answer involves creating preferred status in the marketplace. And it is simple.

It is the value that you bring to the marketplace as defined by the market that determines your income level. The formula for increasing your income level is already in place. The only question to ask yourself is whether or not you are using this formula, this standard of excellence, to improve your economic position in life. In professional sales, we cannot go to the legislature to ask them to change a law to pay us more. Nor can we organize ourselves as a union and demand higher pay using the threat of striking as our leverage. To move up the income ladder we must increase our value as perceived by both our employers and our customers. The tactics and strategies in this book are designed to help improve your value so that you can begin to enjoy the extraordinary life that the profession of selling offers.

The Formula

When I speak to audiences throughout North America I am routinely asked, "What is the formula for success?" A number of years ago I was introduced to a formula that was designed to create wealth. My friend, Michael Smythe, introduced me to this formula:

D.V. (Distinctive Value) x Q. (Quantity) = W. (Wealth)

I took Michael's formula and applied it to our business model and the results were remarkable. I then introduced it to some of my clients, again with the same results. If ever there was a magic formula–this was it!

With more experience my confidence in Michael's formula increased. I began looking for ways to apply it to my sales process. Over the next several years, I expanded the formula. The result of that re-engineering was as follows:

(E.V. [Expected Value] + D.V. [Distinctive Value]) x T. (Trust) = P.S. (Preferred Status)

We will cover the Preferred Status formula in more detail in section three of this book. Simply put, Expected Value is what the customer expects to receive from your products or service. Expected Value is what your core business offering aims to be. It is sufficient to say that your core business offering must match your customer's expectations. If it does not, then Preferred Status can never be achieved regardless.

Instead I want to focus on that element of Michael Smythe's formula called DV or Distinctive Value. Most companies that I work with bring value to the marketplace in some way. The problem with many of them, however, is that their value is just not distinctive. If I can find comparable products or services elsewhere, then your business offering is not distinctive. And if your business offering is not distinctive, then you should be asking yourself a key question: "Will your customers pay a premium for a product or service that is unique, rare, or precious?"

The answer to that question is found when we take a closer look at the formula. You can forget for the time being about the W or Wealth, because Wealth is the end result. It is on the other side of the equals sign. Many sales organizations make the mistake of focusing on the end result rather than on the process that will get you the end result. The Wealth will grow automatically if you employ effective Distinctive Value or Quantity strategies.

The first question I ask my clients is: "Do you have Distinctive Value problems, do you have Quantity problems (marketing), or do you have both?"

Distinctive Value

Most companies bring value to the marketplace; it is just not distinctive. If your company's value is not distinctive, then the only way you can grow your business is to expand your market share or your

Quantity. This is why you continually read in the newspaper about company "X" merging with company "Y". Because many companies lack Distinctive Value, they do not create enough Wealth for their stakeholders and must, therefore, take other measures to grow. Lacking Distinctive Value, customers often will go elsewhere for their products, especially during competitive price promotions. Consequently, it takes years to increase their piece of the market pie. When this occurs, larger and smarter companies that have the financial resources will take over other companies and with a stroke of the pen increase their market share. It does not take a rocket scientist to pull this off, just a lot of money.

Companies that focus on Distinctive Value strategies, however, easily differentiate themselves from the competition and expand their business by virtue of the unique products and services they offer. They expand their Quantity through marketing initiatives and distinctive product offerings.

There are two types of Distinctive Value. The first is *Product* or *Service-based* Distinctive Value. These are the products and services that are unique to your company. The challenge with a product or service-based Distinctive Value is that it has a limited shelf life. In today's marketplace technological advances occur competitively in real time. Competitors will often make similar advances at the same time, or if not, it takes only days, weeks or months to catch up with a competitor's advantage. Any competitive advantage that is created through product or service-based Distinctive Value is short-term at best. Competitors will bring out a "me-too" product or service, or even worse, they will often leap ahead with an innovation that supercedes the technology. Then we are caught scrambling to catch up to them.

Think for a moment about your own industry. When your company comes out with a new product or service, what is the average shelf life of that advantage? Three months, six months, maybe a year at best? Rarely do advances remain elite for a longer period.

Success based on technological advances is also usually short-lived unless it is leveraged to create other markets. Remember Apple Computer? They went from zero to a billion dollars in one year. Why did they become so popular so quickly? Their product-based Distinctive Value was ease of use. They created the graphical interface.

A few years later, Microsoft enters the marketplace in a big way with Windows, also a graphical interface. Apple's product-based Distinctive Value disappears. Microsoft puts their operating system on all new IBM computers being sold. They grab the Quantity and guess what? They are still the market leaders, not so much because of their Distinctive Value (although they have continued to leverage their strengths successfully), but because of their distribution or Quantity strategy. Apple has recently revamped their Distinctive Value Strategy with slick product designs and are expanding their Quantity with more retail outlets.

Federal Express and UPS provide another example. A number of years ago Federal Express came out with PowerShip. PowerShip was a software product that would allow customers to track their shipments directly. Rather than call an 800 number and wait to talk to a customer service representative, customers could log into the system and find out in real time the exact location of their packages. A short time later, UPS launched UPS OnLine, which essentially did the same thing, thereby successfully neutralizing the Distinctive Value created by Federal Express that was threatening their business.

Another example: VHS and Beta video cassette recorders. VHS was created first; Beta was the innovation, the improvement. In an internal meeting somewhere in the corporate boardrooms of Sony, some ill-fated person suggested that Sony keep the Beta format for itself because it was the better technology. As a result, Matsushita wisely chose to focus on their Quantity and quickly cross-licensed VHS to several other manufacturers. Whenever I ask audiences which is a better technology, they routinely respond with Beta. Think about it. We are all using an inferior technology because of a marketing or Quantity strategy. Interestingly, the broadcast industry still uses Beta as the standard for recording technology.

As another example, in recent years we saw Netscape come into the marketplace with their web browser. It had great Distinctive Value. Their Quantity strategy was simple. They provided it for free on the web. It quickly became the industry standard and Netscape enjoys about 65 percent of the browser market. In their case, both their Distinctive Value and their Quantity was strong.

So here is another lesson we can learn from these examples. Even if our competitors have a better widget than we do, even if they have better technology than we do, we can still win if we have a better Quantity or marketing strategy. Obviously I am not suggesting that you give up on research and development. Product and service innovation is imperative in today's marketplace. What I am saying is this: Don't put all your eggs in one basket. Remember this rule. When it comes to product or service-based Distinctive Value there will always be a company that will come along and do it quicker, cheaper, and better than yours.

In other words, eat your own lunch before your competitors do!

Companies that fail to continually innovate or improve their products and services face the risk of not surviving. You would be quite shocked if you could review today the Forbes Fortune 500 list of 1975. Seventy-five percent of those Fortune 500 companies do not exist anymore. These companies do not exist because they failed to maintain either their Distinctive Value or their Quantity or both.

Service-based Distinctive Value

If you sell products and services that are commodities and do not have Distinctive Value by their nature, then you must provide your Distinctive Value through service. A whole genre of successful companies developed in the eighties and nineties based primarily on providing the consumer with an exceptional service experience. In other words, they provided service-based Distinctive Value. Nordstrom, Wal-Mart, Starbucks, Federal Express, and Amazon.com are just a few examples of service providers that have become preferred in their marketplace by focusing on an exceptional consumer experience and providing service-based Distinctive Value.

Michael Smythe gives an excellent example of how service-based Distinctive Value can give you competitive advantage. Assume your car is in need of repair. You take it down to the repair depot and they tell you something like this: "Okay, we need three hours with your car and you have two choices. First choice: We will give you a ride down to your place of employment and pick you up when your car is finished. Second choice: You can sit in our waiting room, eat our donuts, drink our coffee and read our magazines. It will cost about $150 dollars to repair your vehicle."

What choice would you make in this case? Would you get a ride to work or would you sit and eat the donuts? You probably have had an experience like this at some point in your life. In fact, even the offering of a ride to your place of employment is a service experience not everybody has received. Thus, you may even consider this to be exceptional. But I can tell you that this would be considered a standard offering in today's marketplace.

A new guy comes into town–me! Michael's Auto and Repair. And this is my service pitch for your business: I will come to your home tonight and pick up your car. My team will work on it all night and we will have it back in your driveway at 6:00 a.m. with keys and paperwork in the mailbox. But it is going to cost you $165, a $15 premium.

Here is the million dollar question: Would you pay the $15 premium? I bet the answer is "yes". How much more would you pay? When I ask my audiences this question, there are many who would gladly pay a $25 to $50 premium for this service. This is a significant learning that is worth emphasizing. For a commodity product or service, why are you are willing to pay a 10 percent, 20 percent or even a 30 percent premium? What did I do differently from my competitors? I provided you with service-based Distinctive Value, even though my product, fixing your car, is not unique. I simply identified your stress and made that stress go away, better than my competitors.

Now let us go back to the car repair scenario for a moment. In the first example, let us say you chose to have the repair shop give you a ride to work and pick you up when your car was ready. Later that day you are having lunch with one of your buddies. Are you having this conversation? "You will never guess what happened to me today! I took my car in for repair and they gave me a ride to work and they are going to pick me up when the car is ready. Can you believe it? Am I ever fortunate!" No, probably not. Are you even talking about it? I don't think so.

Let us look at the second example, where I am providing you with service-based Distinctive Value. I come to your home, pick up your car and deliver it back to you fully repaired first thing in the morning. You walk out and there is your car, fixed, ready to go, and maybe I even included a wash service. As you sit later in the day having lunch with your work associates, are you saying anything? Are you telling your friends and associates about the service? You bet, unless you are one of those people that likes to hide a good thing from your friends for fear that it will limit your access to it. My guess is that you are recommending me to your friends and making yourself look good in the process. In fact, I would count on that occurring to help build my business. This is the best form of advertising on the planet, which we call word-of-mouth advertising or advocacy, and it is a natural result of providing Distinctive Value. And of course, the beauty of Distinctive Value is that it substantially increases the end result, which you will remember from our formula, is Wealth.

Knowledge-based Distinctive Value

When you focus on product or service-based Distinctive Value, the bar will always get raised. You will have to continually innovate to stay ahead of the pack. Competition will get faster, stronger, and more efficient, and it will force you to do the same if you want to compete. Companies that fail to keep up with industry innovations will ultimately fail. There is a second form of Distinctive Value, however, that I believe will give you a competitive advantage for a much longer period of time and will leave your competitors wondering what happened. This is what is called knowledge-based Distinctive Value, and it will set your company apart from the rest of the pack.

About a hundred years ago we were operating in the agricultural age. We moved from the agricultural age to the industrial age with the advent of machines. Machines made us more efficient and made us stronger, faster and more productive than we had ever been before. From there we advanced into the technological age. This change was fueled by the discovery of the personal computer, and the technological age became quickly valued for its ability to make us smarter, and again, more efficient. Now, however, we are in the age of information or knowledge. And this age, too, promises to provide us with new and more advantages, primarily through the creation, management and dissemination of information or knowledge.

Here are some examples of companies that have gained competitive advantage using a knowledge-based Distinctive Value strategy. My company, Summit Learning Systems, markets products and services to sales and service companies throughout North America. Our key targets are companies with an active sales force. The primary individual for our contact at these companies is the sales manager or the vice-president of sales and marketing.

As with service-based Distinctive Value, one of the questions we ask our company contacts when we begin to work for them is: "What are their market needs?" "What issues cause them continual stress?" We also ask the same question of our target individual. What can we do to alleviate the stress and business concern of the sales manager or vice-president?

To answer these questions requires us to examine certain assumptions to determine whether they are valid. For one, we usually assume that the sales manager or vice-president is responsible for keeping the sales team motivated, meeting or exceeding sales targets week after week, and ensuring long-term profitable growth. And we assume that they likely do not have enough time in the day to accomplish these tasks, along with the host of other tasks they are likely required to perform within their jobs.

So, to alleviate this concern and stress we take specific action. We produce a report called the "Sales Tip of the Week." This is a one-page document that we electronically distribute to sales managers or vice presidents every week. Sunday evening our computers electronically push thousands of faxes and emails out to our selected target markets that have accepted our free subscriptions. The sales tips are sitting on the sales managers desk first thing Monday morning so that they can use them in their meetings throughout the week. The sales managers love them because they are always in need of fresh and practical ideas to motivate or inspire their teams.

We love them because every week we are in front of our target market with great tips on how to improve sales performance. Whenever our target company has a sales conference or requires sales training, guess who they call first? The company that is fresh on their

"Like the principle of karma, or the Golden Rule, we create positive business karma, and our clients reward us with their loyalty, their trust, and their business."

Monday morning minds–us. Rather than send our sales team in month after month saying "give me, give me, give me," we send them our best information on a weekly basis to address the issues they face day in and day out. In other words, we provide value on a weekly basis. We operate from a contribution perspective, rather than a consumption perspective. This practice reaps us all kinds of short-term and long-term rewards. Like the principle of karma, or the Golden Rule, we create positive business karma, and our clients reward us with their loyalty, their trust, and their business.

I recently received a phone call from the President of an international medical diagnostic company. The conversation went something like this: "Mr. Vickers, this is ..." and he introduced himself. "We have been receiving your sales tips for a number of months now and our sales people find them useful. We are having a conference in a major resort in a few months, and we'd be honored if you would come to the resort and speak to our national sales team. We will, of course, take care of all of your travel, accommodations and expenses. We would like you to stay with us at the resort."
I expressed my appreciation to him, and I agreed to go. He then asked, "By the way, what is your fee?" I told him and he didn't flinch a bit. He simply said, "No problem, we look forward to having you."

That is what I call being *preferred*. This company is sent literally hundreds of proposals from speakers all over the world and they selected me. Why? Because I worried first about addressing their needs, before addressing one of mine. I have used this strategy successfully with many of today's leading companies and have achieved the same results. What was the key differentiating point? What set me apart from the competitors? It was the knowledge-based Distinctive Value that I was giving away for free.

The questions you should ask yourself about knowledge-based Distinctive Value are, "Will your clients or customers pay a premium for information or knowledge? Will they pay a premium for applied knowledge? Will they pay a premium for wisdom?" I am going to suggest to you that knowledge is the ultimate currency and they will indeed pay for it.

Let us look at another example and then you can decide. Every month I select a Book of the Month. I carefully dissect the book, marking it up with notes in the margin, key points following a bright idea, and highlighting sentences, paragraphs and sections that I believe are innovative, new and insightful. Then I prepare an executive summary of the book outlining its applicable concepts. I then purchase several dozen books, hand them off to my support staff and get them to mark up the books exactly the same way that I have. They write in the margins, highlight key points, and identically copy what I have done in my prototype. As a rule, I like to send a book a quarter to a major decision-maker with each of my top clients. The company president or executive that I am sending the book to may or may not have read the book I send them. However, I know for certain that they haven't dissected the book like I have. If they are like most executives, who have little reading time, they usually read my executive summary and then put the book on their bookshelf with the others.

Now let us look at this example a little more closely. Executives do not have a lot of time to do the reading. Therefore, I am saving them time, and I am making them smarter by providing them with pertinent points from leading educational material. Secondly, I know that my competitors are not doing this. So this service of providing Distinctive Value through knowledge sets me apart from the competition. I am providing leading edge information that helps my clients and potential clients. I am a valuable resource to them. Each contribution that I make adds value to the business relationship and further insulates me from any competitive erosion.

Here is one last case study. There are three manufacturers that make widgets. They all sell their widgets to a national retailer. All three manufacturers have similar products. The retailer gives about a third of the business to each of them just to keep things fair and competitive.

Manufacturer A, our client, says, "We are frustrated. We come up with a new widget, and our competitors come up with a new one. We lower our prices, and they lower their prices. Help us! How do we get a bigger piece of the pie in our market?"

The first question we ask is, "What is your customers' stress?" "We don't know," comes the answer. How are you going to find out? Ask your customers! "Hey target market, what's driving you crazy?"

"We will tell you what's driving us crazy. You widget manufacturers are driving us crazy. We have problems with delivery, and quality, and we can't compete with the smaller independents. We are thinking of getting out of widgets."

So what do we do now to help our client?

We spend the next five months developing a marketing strategy to drive customers into stores to buy widgets. Not just our client's widgets, but all widgets.

Five months later we ask our client, "How is it going?"

"Great!" is the reply. "We have more customer traffic than ever, but our sales people aren't trained proficiently to close the deal."

So what do we do next?

We spend the next six months training their people how to sell widgets more effectively. But we train them how to sell all widgets, not just our client's widgets. One year later, our client has a 65 percent share of the market, and the rest is split primarily between the other two competing national brands.

What happened here? How did our client grow their business at the expense of their competitors? They did so by exceeding expectations. Providing detailed marketing plans to help sell widgets and providing sales training on how to sell widgets is not something the customers of our client expected.

Assume you are the buyer from a national retailer and you have three sales reps coming to see you each month. Every time the sales rep from Company A shows up they bring you information or knowledge-based Distinctive Value that helps eliminate your stress. Would this action influence your buying decision? If the price of the competing products were the same as the price of the products of Company A, would you have a preference? I bet you would.

Whenever you show up somewhere to sell a product, the expectation is that you will wave your company flag and describe your company's products in detail. This is not exceeding expectations; it is simply meeting expectations. In some cases, it may even be falling below expectations and contributing to the problems you should be trying to solve. You can exceed expectations, however, if you bring with you on every sales call knowledge-based Distinctive Value that addresses and eases the stress of the customer you are visiting. This is providing a level of service they do not expect.

The rule is simple. If you want to meet your success expectations, simply meet the expectations of your customers or clients. However, if you wish to exceed your own success expectations, then you must exceed theirs. If you consistently contribute to your customer's or client's business, even when it has little to do with your own core competencies, then you will exceed their expectations and will become a needed and valuable part of their business.

Professional, Knowledge-based Distinctive Value

There are two types of knowledge-based Distinctive Value, *personal* and *professional*. The following are some examples of professional, knowledge-based Distinctive Value:

- **Technical books.** Prepare technical summaries based on books related to your industry. Most people do not take the time to read books, but they will read a summary.

- **Web sites.** Prepare a list of websites for your customers that are significant to their business.

Anything you can do to save them time is a bonus. Remember that time is a currency. Saving time saves money.

- **Technical tip of the week.** Consider sending your customers a technical tip of the week via fax or email. We send out thousands of these tips every week to our client and prospect base. We send them our best knowledge on a weekly basis.

- **Audio cassettes.** Put together an audio tape that includes a description of technological changes within their industry. For example, one of our clients distributes an audio tape every week to their customers with the latest changes that are affecting the industry. Most people do not have enough time to read, but they do drive around in their vehicles all day. By providing your customers or clients with audio cassettes related to their industry or market, you can create a virtual "University on Wheels" that keeps your clients up to speed.

- **Newsletters.** Many of our clients send out newsletters. The best ones are those that talk about them, not you! Consider featuring some of your clients or information related to the personal and/or professional challenges that they have successfully overcome.

- **Articles.** Collect articles related to your customers' business and send them out on a weekly basis, with a reference to where they can obtain additional information. The leading thinkers in any given area are constantly staying ahead of new written materials addressing related topics of concern.

- **Seminars or technical lunches.** Organizing and hosting seminars or technical lunches is a very powerful strategy. Many of our clients gain competitive advantage by preparing industry seminars. These seminars are delivered at breakfast or lunch meetings.

Personal, Knowledge-based Distinctive Value

Do not underestimate the power of providing *personal, knowledge-based* Distinctive Value to your customers. It can be a very effective way of closing a deal. Let me give you an example.

A few years ago, I was in the vice president's office of an international company. The executive I was dealing with was a terrific poker player. Cards to the vest and no facial expressions whatsoever. I was getting absolutely no feedback from our meeting. As we shook hands to say goodbye, I decided to ask a simple question: "Brian, when you are not working ten hours a day, what do you do for fun?"

"I climb mountains," was his response.

"Technical or backpacking," I asked.

"Technical," he responded enthusiastically.

Cha-Ching! I got the information I was looking for. We talked for thirty seconds or so about his mountain climbing adventures. Now he was animated, and he was excited talking about his hobby. I went back to my office, searched my contact manager and found that I had about six other executives who were interested in technical mountain climbing. I then called a famous mountaineer who lives in our city and asked if he would be interested in conducting a workshop for some executives that would hire him as a speaker. He agreed to do the workshop. I called Brian, along with the other six executives, and invited him to the half-day workshop. He enthusiastically accepted. The event was terrific, and everyone had a great time. Several weeks later we closed the deal. It was one of the biggest contracts we have ever sold.

There is an interesting epilogue to this story. A number of months went by and I was having lunch with a consultant friend of mine. He congratulated me on the deal. His next comment was even more telling. He asked, "What do you guys have on Brian over at company X?"

I acted dumb. "What do you mean?"

"I was in the meeting where your company was

"It is important to remember that people always buy first because of emotion. Then they justify their purchases with logic. How are you selling your products and services? Emotionally or logically?"

awarded the contract. I have never seen Brian so enthusiastic as he advocated for your company! "

"It must be the quality of our services," I explained with a huge grin on my face.

Do not underestimate the power of investing in the personal side of your clients or customers. I could fill an entire book with examples of the many contracts we have landed because of the personal, knowledge-based Distinctive Value strategy.

I fly airplanes for a hobby. I have been flying for about twenty years. Try calling my office and setting an appointment to sell me something. You will never get past the gatekeepers. Call me up and invite me to fly in a simulator for a Boeing 777 for thirty minutes and you just made a new best friend. Why? Because now you have gotten to my passions, my emotions. It is important to remember that people always buy first because of emotion. Then they justify their purchases with logic. How are you selling your products and services? Emotionally or logically? When you focus on personal, knowledge-based Distinctive Value, you create an opportunity to establish an emotional connection. You must establish the emotional connection if you are to become preferred over the long run.

Here are some ideas of activities you can facilitate for your customers, depending upon their interests, that will provide the personal type of Distinctive Value we have been discussing:

Hobbies and Interests:

- Sports
- Family history
- Woodworking
- Sewing
- Cooking
- Animals
- Financial planning
- Educational activities
- Reading

- Outdoor activities
- Bird watching
- Decorating
- Gardening
- Traveling
- Wine making
- Building a business
- Star gazing

Remember too, that nothing is more important to most people than their families. Take the time to get to know the names of your client's partners, their children, their pets, and get to know their interests. Taking interest in the things that are most valuable to your clients will help you become a friend as well as a business associate.

Providing Distinctive Value

Whether or not you should focus on providing your clients or customers with professional or personal knowledge-based Distinctive Value is in large part a value judgment that you have to make. In either case, however, there are a couple of steps you should follow to determine how to proceed. First, identify your target market. Be very clear about who it is you think will get value from what it is that you can provide. Second, learn enough about them and their needs that you understand their business challenges and anything that is causing stress in their life–whether it is professional or personal stress. Be careful with your assumptions. If you are not sure, ask them. Third, ask yourself what knowledge-based Distinctive Value could you give that they would find useful. Make sure that the knowledge is pertinent to their core business or to one of their needs, professional or personal. Finally, begin the process of steadily supplying them Distinctive Value that will address the needs, challenges and opportunities that you have identified.

One important word about Distinctive Value. Providing Distinctive Value is in essence the building block that you are using to build a bridge (or relationship) with your clients and customers. If Distinctive Value could be considered the bricks that become a part of that bridge, trust is the mortar–the glue that holds those bricks and bridges together. Remember that in all relationships trust is a multiplier. The more your customers trust you, the bigger piece of the pie they will be willing to give you. You can measure this by simply taking a hard look at how many other competitors your customers buy from on terms essentially equal to yours. If there are no other strategic reasons why they are doing so (e.g. location) then perhaps there is an issue of trust. Perhaps they are afraid to put "all of their eggs in your basket." If so, find out why and try to overcome the issue.

"The strategy behind knowledge-based Distinctive Value is that you are coming from a position of contribution rather than simply seeking a sale."

Traditional sales processes can build trust over time, for they all focus on the importance of the relationship to one degree or another. However, the strategies and tactics I will share with you in this book will help you build relationships of trust more quickly and more deeply than your competitors. The reason for this is quite simple. The strategy behind knowledge-based Distinctive Value is that you are coming from a position of contribution rather than simply seeking a sale. When you call on an account you are not positioning things to get what you want. Instead, you are bringing them value as your customers or prospects define it. You are positioning yourself to help them get what they want. This practice will build trust rapidly. Remember when you demonstrate to them that you care more about their business than you seemingly care about your own, you build trust.

Preferred Status

Let us talk some more about Preferred Status. This is, after all, why we are learning about providing Distinctive Value to your customers. All of us as service or product providers seek to achieve Preferred Status with our customers and clients. So let us learn more about this and what it really means.

There are three levels of Preferred Status. The first is *Loyalty*. This one makes me nervous. We all have customers whom we would classify as loyal. I believe, however, that it is dangerous for any organization to

believe that it has loyal or satisfied customers.
Experience teaches me that so-called "loyal customers"
can often be easily lured away with price. That is, they
are loyal to you providing that you are price
competitive. This is especially true if you gained the
customer or client through discounting against a
competitor. Remember, if they come to you for price,
they will leave you for price. So, rely on the loyalty of
your dog, not your customer. Unless your customer or
client is a Golden Retriever, always be cautious.

The second level of Preferred Status is *Advocacy*. This
is where your customer is advocating for you. They are
giving you word of mouth advertising for free. Most of
us would agree that this is the most effective form of
advertising. We, in essence, become referable.
When we are referred, price is generally not an issue.
The parties to whom we have been referred and the
referring party are both likely to pay a premium to use
our products or services. As sales and service
organizations we should be continually striving to
move our customers from loyalty to advocacy.

Once we have them advocating on our behalf, we
should then develop strategies and processes that will
move them to the third and final level of Preferred
Status: *Insistence*.

Insistence means you are truly preferred. Companies
that enjoy this level of status with their customers
enjoy high profit margins and have real market

security. Your customers insist on doing business with you and no one else will do. It takes a lot of work to achieve this level of preferred status. You must be providing significant Distinctive Value, both professional and personal, and you must enjoy the highest level of trust with your clients and customers.

The Five Customer Values

You can simplify the work required to achieve "insistence status" if you understand what is important to your clients; if you understand what they really value. In general, there are five *Customer Values* that will drive the priorities of your clients.

The first customer value is the obvious one – *Money*. Most sales professionals are experts on this one. They understand the financial issues, and they are acutely aware of the value of money in any business transaction. The problem that most of them make, however, is that when they get into a competitive situation they immediately drop their price. Inevitably this leads to lower profit margins and a loss of value. Sales professionals, to be truly effective, must learn more effective ways of selling than price discounting. Unless the goal of your company is to be the low cost provider in your industry, price discounting will hurt the perceived value of you and your company, and therefore should be avoided at all costs. Rather than ask the question, "Should we lower our prices to be more competitive," you should ask the question, "What

"Rather than ask the question, "Should we lower our prices to be more competitive," you should ask the question, "What services do we need to provide to incentivize the customer to pay us a premium?"

services do we need to provide to incentivize the customer to pay us a premium?" In most cases, you are better off establishing your relationship by providing better value, rather than a better price.

The second customer value is the value of the new millennium-*Time*. Will your clients or customers pay a premium to save time? A number of years ago we were remodeling a home. As part of the remodel I wanted a home theatre built into a recreation room. The building of this room was finally completed on a Friday. I had all of the latest electronics in this room. I had the big screen, the surround sound stereo, and of course the top quality speakers. The room was looking great with one exception. There was no couch. I had forgotten to plan for the couch. So I hurried that day down to a national brand furniture store in my city. I found a couch that was suitable and here is how the conversation went with the salesman:

"How much is this couch?" I asked.

"$1800" was the reply.

"When can you deliver it?"

"We can deliver it next Wednesday," the salesman replied.

"Oh no!" I said. "The boys are coming over Sunday evening to watch the big game. I need it sometime in the next 48 hours."

"Sorry sir, we can't do it that fast," came his reply.

"How much are you going to charge me for delivery?" I asked.

"$50," he answered.

"I will give you $100 if you can get it there in the next 48 hours," I joyously exclaimed.

"Sorry sir, I can't do it," he responded.

"I will give you $150 dollars," I argued, not wanting to be defeated.

"Sorry sir, it wouldn't matter how much you paid me, we can't do it that fast," came his final reply.

Yeah, whatever, I thought to myself.

I left the store and went down the street to their number one competitor.

Again I found a couch that would be suitable. I asked the salesman, "When can you deliver it?"

"When would you like it delivered?" was his response.

"I need it in the next 48 hours," I exclaimed. "The boys are coming over for the big game Sunday night."

"How about tonight after dinner, let's say 6:30 p.m.," came his response.

"I love you man!" I responded. "You complete me."

"How much are you going to charge me for delivery?" I added.

"No charge sir, it's included in the price," he responded.

Would I have paid a delivery charge? Of course I would have. Enthusiastically. How much would I have paid? Who knows, but I would have paid something. Save time for someone, and you do not necessarily need to save them money. Price becomes a non-factor in such situations. What premium are you getting for time? Airlines are great examples of capitalizing on the currency of time. When you book a trip in advance you take advantage of your planning skills and you pay a cheaper price for your ticket. When you walk up to the airline counter and ask for a ticket that leaves on the next flight you will pay a premium. Even on the discount airlines you will pay a premium. The value of time, therefore, commands a higher price premium. Other companies do this as well. Federal Express charges you a premium for earlier delivery. You pay a premium for high speed internet. In the evaluation of your business services, make sure that you effectively employ the currency of time in the value proposition that you offer.

The third customer value is *Prestige*. Will your clients or customers pay a premium to feel special? You can buy a Timex watch for $50 that will tell you the time and date, and it is a pretty good watch. You can also buy a watch for $5000 that does the same thing. $50 of that watch goes to the creation of the time and date function. Where does the other $4950 go? To materials and an image that make you feel special, that provide you with a certain degree of prestige. Why do we drive the cars that we drive? Why do we live where we live? Why do we wear what we wear? Why do we eat where we eat? Why do we vacation where we vacation? The answer to these questions often involves the value of prestige. What premium are you getting for prestige? Make your customer or client feel special and they will be willing to pay a premium for your product or service.

The fourth customer value is that of ***Reliability***. Many of your clients or customers will pay a premium for a reliable product or service. They will pay more for quality, more for guaranteed delivery, and more for a product that will not break down as often as another. That is the reason why companies such as Levi Strauss & Co. have been so successful around the world. You always know when you buy a pair of Levis that you are getting a good quality, reliable pair of jeans–every time. Ford and Chevrolet have also spent billions of dollars ensuring that their trucks deliver the customer value of reliability. They know that reliability is an important value to their truck-buying customers, and they know their customers will pay more if reliability and quality are ensured. What premium are you getting for reliability?

The fifth and final customer value is *Knowledge*. Will your customers pay you a premium for knowledge? Absolutely. Knowledge in my opinion is the ultimate currency. That is why knowledge-based Distinctive Value works so effectively. Increased and superior knowledge can lead to more money, time, prestige, and quality. Knowledge is the currency that can facilitate and enhance the delivery of all the other currencies. That is why I believe it is the most important of the currencies. That is why doctors, lawyers, accountants, tax specialists, consultants, educational institutions, and the entire internet industry, can command such high value in our marketplace. They all provide enhanced or increased knowledge to their clients. What premium are you getting for knowledge?

Many sales professionals, when faced with a competitive situation immediately attack the price of the product or service. Management hears things like, "We have to lower our prices to remain competitive," or "If we could just meet our competitor's prices we can close the deal," or "We just have to lower our prices a bit and we will get the contract." So you are stuck playing the price game.

The next time you are faced with a challenging competitive situation, conduct an analysis of your business and assess how many of the five values you are actually providing to your clients or customers. Try to think of ways to employ all of the five customer values into your sales process, instead of just thinking

"Price is never the issue, unless it is the issue. And when price is the issue, it is the only issue."

about money and price. In survey after survey of customer needs and priorities, price shows up fourth, seventh, ninth, as the primary driver for making the purchasing decision. Yet we still see so many companies and sales professionals that remain focused on price as their primary strategy for responding to competitive pressure. Remember this: "Price is never the issue, unless it is the issue. And when price is the issue, it is the only issue." If it is not the issue, then look to one of the four other currencies to provide value to your customers or clients.

To summarize, let us revisit for a moment what we have learned in this section. First, we learned that if we are going to move up the income ladder personally or as an organization, we must bring value to the market as the market defines that value, not as we do. Second, we discussed the importance of our Distinctive Value strategies, both the service-based or product-based strategy, and the knowledge-based strategy. We discussed the importance of providing knowledge-based Distinctive Value, and providing our customers and clients with information that will ease and resolve their issues and concerns. We also discussed the importance of our Quantity or marketing strategies, and the value of developing a process that will allow us to integrate our core business plan with a strategy for marketing and providing Distinctive Value. And finally, we reviewed the concept of customer value and took a closer look at the five customer values or currencies. We concluded that we must understand the currencies or values that are most important to our clients and customers and ensure that we are addressing those values in our business propositions.

Now we will take a closer look at the sales process.

THE SALES PROCESS

In today's marketplace, companies have developed processes for the delivery of their products, accounting, and customer service. It surprises me, however, that many of them lack a sales process. Routinely I ask sales professionals representing a full spectrum of industries to outline for me their company's sales process. Often I get blank stares.

I believe that any company, organization, or individual with the financial ability to purchase your product or service will buy from you if you apply an effective sales process. Unfortunately, many of today's sales professionals try to wing it and win business by the seat of their pants or with their award-winning personality. That will work some of the time, but if you create a sales process and execute that process effectively, you will consistently win a greater share of the business.

Let me illustrate what I mean when I talk about a sales process. This is our sales process and you can make the appropriate adjustments to fit your business:

We start with a prospect funnel. Nothing revolutionary here, we simply research all companies in our selected market niche or market segment. We then identify key individuals within those companies who make or influence the buying decisions. Our Education Coordinators (our salespeople) make their initial contact with the key influencers on the telephone.

They have only one objective when they call. They will not try to sell our services on the phone, they will not give the proverbial feature dump; their goal is only to sell an appointment.

We call these appointments "briefings" (brief means short and sweet). The purpose of the briefing is primarily to find out more about them, identify some of their personal and professional stresses, and to learn how they operate their business. We also give the prospect a little bit of information.

The next step in our process is to sell the prospect on what we call our "proof in advance seminar." This is where we come into their facility and put on a 45-minute presentation for their sales team. The presentation is not a commercial; it is our best 45 minutes. At the time we schedule the "proof in advance" seminar, we also schedule a follow-up de-briefing with the prospect to review the feedback from our initial presentation.

Notice that there are a number of activities or events that are executed in a certain order. It is important to follow the process one step at a time, and one before the other. Think of it as a recipe! You have to add ingredients in a certain order if you are going to get the desired results. The point is that you should have an identifiable step for each part of the sales process.

If everything goes as planned, our process works effectively and we make the sale. We also have built-in contingency plans every step of the way when things do not go as planned. When our sales professionals run into an obstacle, they do not have to think about what to do next. Our sales process will give them the next step and all of the possible variations. The process is graphically represented in a flow chart, and it allows for all kinds of possibilities.

Most sales professionals understand what to do if they get a "yes". The problem comes when they get a "no". What are you going to do when the prospect says no? Sales trainers have taught for years that selling is a numbers game. If you get a no, move on to the next call and the next until you get a yes. I call this the "low-hanging fruit" model. You walk around and pick off the easy business. The problem with this strategy is that your competitors are doing the same thing. No one wants to take the time to get out the "Distinctive Value Ladder," put it up against the tree and pick where no one else is picking.

Sales processes are never complete or completed; they are dynamic. They must be flexible, and they require continuous refinement. Look for bottlenecks and inefficiencies and then make the adjustments. You will end up with a sales process that will help you win more business and give you a competitive advantage for a long time.

The Impending Event

A key element of any sales process is to create an impending event. An impending event is simply an action step that the prospect can anticipate. Impending events are what drive the sales process. In our sales process example, the "proof in advance" seminar is our first impending event. After that presentation, our next impending event is a de-brief session with the decision-maker.

Each impending event is communicated to the prospect. Sometimes we send reminder faxes, emails or letters depending on the interval between impending events. There are a number of benefits derived from using this strategy. First of all, it demonstrates to the prospect that you are professional and pay attention to the details. If they see you executing your follow-up strategies effectively, they assume that you will handle your products and services in the same way. This process builds confidence and trust.

The impending event strategy works because of the psychology behind it. Our conditioning as children and well into adulthood is built around impending events. It might be Christmas, a birthday, a vacation, a move, the release of a new movie that you have been waiting to see, a new book, a job promotion, or a year end bonus. All of these events are designed to get you to anticipate the event and to create something to which you can look forward.

Imagine the advantage that you would have over your competition if you took the time to create impending events that would cause your prospect or client to actually look forward to your next visit. One of our impending event tactics is to send out the "Sales Tip of the Week" as I spoke of earlier. They help prompt our clients to take constructive actions to improve their own sales processes, while at the same time help to create greater interest in the sales concepts and strategies that we are teaching.

This practice facilitates our sales process and creates "impending events" for our subsequent visits. I have discovered that the impending event strategy is not only effective but fun as well. A well-designed sales process contains many impending events.

The Traditional Approach

There are many sales processes and there are many variations of those processes. Typically, I run into this process or some variation of it:

Traditional Model of Selling

10% Rapport — 20% Qualifying — 30% Features & Benefits — 40% Closing

Step 1. Develop rapport. This is where we show up in front of the prospect, shake hands, introduce ourselves and look around their office to try and find something to talk about to warm them up. We have been taught that we must become expert rapport builders if we are going to be successful. We operate on the premise that if they do not like us they will not buy from us.

Step 2. Qualifying. We ask qualifying questions to determine if they have the ability to purchase our products and services. How much business do they do? Who are they currently buying from? We are trying to uncover some of their needs so that we can provide solutions for them.

Step 3. Features and benefits. This is where we get to tell them how cool our products and services are and why we are number one. We tell them why we are the biggest and the best. We then pull out that glossy brochure that highlights us as a company, our products and what we can do for them. Essentially this is where we beat our chests and make jungle noises.

Step 4. The Close. Not long after the "feature dump," our hands start to sweat. We know that the time to ask for the order is fast approaching. This is the step that separates the sales champions from the order takers. This is the "Close." The close is the time when we get to go into our selling toolbox and pull out that sure-fire close that has got us this far in life. (We might even have many sure-fire closes in our toolbox, just in case the first one does not work).

This is the traditional sales process I have seen used thousands of times by thousands of sales professionals throughout North America. It is the way many sell. Does it work? Yes, it works. Just not well! During my presentations to audiences on this topic, I usually get someone from the audience to role-play their sales process with me. I do this over 100 times a year, with a myriad of different companies representing most industries. Again and again I get the same process or at least a slight variation of it. Sales trainers all over North America have been teaching this process for years. It does work. The problem is that most buyers have seen it so many times that they understand how to effectively defend against it.

You might have experienced a certain amount of success with a variation of this approach yourself. Keep this one in your toolbox. There are times when it is useful, for instance, when you are only interested in the low-hanging fruit. There are some customers for whom you do not want to invest a lot of time and energy. This approach can work effectively when this type of situation arises. However, I am not interested in the business you get using this process, because you are already getting this business. Rather, I am interested in helping you get the business you are not able to get using this process.

Let us call the first process the traditional model of selling. We call it traditional because of its widespread use and its basic effectiveness. It operates under the assumption that if you play by the numbers you will get a number of hits each time that you step up to the plate to bat. Ultimately it means that you will get the order if you are in the right place at the right time. However, one of the drawbacks with this model is that the business is usually not very profitable. Low-hanging fruit business is usually obtained by offering the lowest price on your products or services, thus diminishing your profit margin.

But what about the fruit that resides higher up in the tree? I believe that if you take the time to go and get a ladder, clear out a place to securely position the ladder and climb up the tree, there is a lot of fruit to pick and not too many competitors. It requires a little more effort, but the payoff is huge because most selling professionals are not willing to invest the extra time. As a consequence, you can usually charge more for your products and services with this type of business, so you increase rather than decrease your profit margins.

The New Model of Selling

The next model I will share with you is designed to allow you to climb higher up the tree. I call it "The New Model of Selling." Let us take a look at its process. You will know how to execute each of the steps in the process. The steps themselves are not new, they are just in a different order and they follow a more simple formula.

New Model of Selling

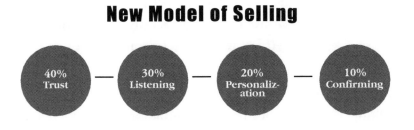

Step 1. Trust. Trust is the foundation of all relationships, personal or organizational. The more that your customers trust you the more they will buy from you. The goal of our sales process is to establish and build trust quicker and better than our competitors. How do we establish trust quickly? How do we get them to lower their resistance barriers with us in the initial meeting or briefing? Here is what I do to establish trust.

"Mr. Prospect, thank you for seeing me. I asked for twenty minutes of your time, just a quick time check, is that still okay with you?" They will usually nod their head with approval. I then proceed with the following:

"In order to help me stay focused and make the best use of your time, I have prepared a number of questions that, with your permission, I would like to ask you." Again, you will likely receive a nod of approval. I then proceed to ask them well thought out questions that I have prepared in advance about their business. Information that will help me identify the opportunities that exist for a business relationship.

Step 2. Listening. You have probably heard the old saying: "God gave us two ears and only one mouth, so we would listen twice as much as we talk." If we are always talking, then we cannot be listening. However, if we are always listening, then who is doing the talking? They are. Listening is an active process that means we are understanding their perspective. It does not mean that we are simply quiet and contemplating the next question we will ask or statement we will make. It means really listening and digesting what it is we are being told.

If they are doing most of the talking it also means that you are likely asking some really good questions. These should not be questions that you have left to chance. I recommend that you develop an inventory of pre-determined questions that include several variations. Do not try and remember them. You will forget them and kick yourself later for not asking the important ones. Simply write them down and refer to your list when asking them. You will appear organized when you do this.

Another important tip when asking questions and listening to responses is resisting the urge to solve their problems right there and then. When they open up and tell you about a problem they are having, do not rush in with a solution, even if it is on the tip of your tongue. Resist, resist, and resist. Just make a note of it. The reason you do not want to rush in with a solution is because you want them to continue talking. You may uncover additional issues that may be even more important and relevant to the solutions that you can provide. If you get side tracked by premature problem solving, you might lose the opportunity to uncover the real dissatisfaction factors they are having.

Step 3. Personalizing. The third step in the new model of selling is called personalizing. This one I cannot help you with at all. This is all about you. This has to do with your life experience, who you are as an individual, and what you can bring to the table. This is about the wisdom that you have gained, the books that you have read, and the tapes that you have listened to. This is your moment of truth. This is where you get to fly solo. This is about your personality. What it does mean, however, is trying your hardest to find those aspects of you that match certain aspects of your potential client or customer. It means finding common ground and customizing or tailoring your sales presentation so that it includes and refers to that common ground. Remember, if they can relate to you they are more likely to buy from you. It also means being creative and using your intelligence to think of new ways for them to think about their business. Undoubtedly, their experience is not your own and you have the unique opportunity to share with them a new perspective that can offer them a fresh look at an old problem. Many business solutions and sales are made this way.

Step 4. Confirming. Finally we move on to the last step of the process. This is the confirmation stage. We should be closing throughout every stage of the process so that when it comes time to actually close the deal, we do not have to close per se, we simply confirm that we are moving ahead. If we have done our job effectively and executed the process properly, then the confirmation stage is the last logical step in the process to secure the business. Because we are bringing solutions to the table that the prospect helped develop they have already bought into the product or services we are offering and now we can take care of the details.

Let us go back to our briefing. After I have asked all of the questions I am going to ask, I then say something like: "Mr. Prospect, I appreciate your openness with me. I would like to go back to my office and prepare some possible solutions that will work for you. I have some ideas that I believe you may find helpful. Let's set a time for me to report back to you with some alternatives that make sense." I then set up the return visit or de-brief and leave.

Notice that I did not try to close on anything but the return visit. Question. What is the trust level like at this point with the prospect? High or low? Probably high. Is it higher than in the traditional sales approach where we try and close the business during the initial visit? Yes. Why is it higher? It is higher because I did not try to close the deal. Today's buyers are so accustomed to seeing the traditional selling process that they are not prepared to handle a true professional. Many sales managers in the audience are usually cringing at this point of my presentations. "What do you mean?" they often think. "You should always be closing!"

Look at how we are appearing to the prospect. We show up, look and act professional, ask some really good questions, and then leave promising to consider carefully how we can resolve some of their issues, all without providing cookie cutter solutions they have already heard many times before. Of course we are going to appear professional! Further, we will be acting like a professional consultant or specialist would act under the same circumstances. If we were to retain a professional consultant and they came into our business, asked a few questions and then had a solution on the tip of their tongue, how would we feel? Likely quite skeptical and we might not have much trust in their solutions. But if they came in, asked some questions and then left without providing a solution, claiming that they wanted to do some additional homework before providing solutions, how would we feel? Which approach would make us feel more comfortable? The answer is, of course, obvious.

When we visit the doctor, in most cases they will ask us some questions, perform some tests and then follow with a diagnosis and a treatment. How would we feel if we walked into the office and they had a prescription already made out for us?

Alternative Solutions

Let us go back to our example for a moment. You go back to your office, work out a number of possible solutions that meet the needs of your client. I like to come up with at least three alternatives that make sense to me: One solution where money is no object, a second solution for less money that will do the job and still has a few bells and whistles added, and a third solution that is low-cost just in case price is the primary issue. In most selling opportunities the client or customer will pick the middle option. Every once in a while they pick the high-end solution and every once in a while they pick the low-cost solution. Customers like to have choices, so I accommodate them with three possible solutions that make sense.

Any solution chosen means your client or customer is moving ahead. As I offer the three solutions to the prospect, I usually say something like, "Based on your responses to my questions, here are three solutions that make sense to me. Solution 1: Money is tight, so we have to do this for the lowest amount possible. Solution 2: I have added some bells and whistles that give you upgrades and increased value. Solution 3: Money is no object, and this is the best solution in the marketplace. Which solution makes most sense to you?" That is it, end of story.

Sometimes they say things like "let me think about it" or "leave it with me for a while." I then respond with, "Great! I will call you later next week and see which solution makes most sense to you." Remember, if the solution makes sense then it makes sense. You do not need fancy closes that will trick the prospect into making a decision–the proof is in the solution! The rule is simple: Do not ever provide a solution that does not make sense. Always prepare three solutions: good, better, and best. All three solutions must make sense. They will pick the low cost solution if money is the issue. Remember again the rule! Money is never the issue, unless it is the issue. And when it is the issue, it is the only issue.

I have shared two basic models of selling with you: the "Traditional Model" and "A New Model of Selling." Notice the subtle differences between them. The "New Model" is designed to build more trust into the process by selling in a more implied or subtle manner. This method will differentiate you from the competition and will give you an advantage.

However, there is a caveat to this new process. Once in a while you will be in the right place at the right time. You will be busy asking great questions and you will hear something like this: "Am I ever glad that you showed up! We are in desperate need of your product and service, how soon can you deliver?" When this lucky day occurs, forget everything that I just shared

"If you will define and apply an effective sales process to your sales activities, you will improve your success ratio dramatically."

with you about the new model of selling and revert back to the traditional model. Close the deal! Remember the low hanging fruit? By special alignment of the stars, or whatever, you happen to be in the right place at the right time. So go ahead and close the deal.

As I mentioned earlier in this section, I believe you can have any account you want if you are willing to pay the price. And I am not talking about discounting. If you will define and apply an effective sales process to your sales activities, you will improve your success ratio dramatically. The sales process that I have introduced to you is based on my experience as well as the experience of the best of the best in the many excellent companies with which I work. It is a process that should be engineered and re-engineered on a regular basis in order to keep it tuned to today's highly dynamic marketplace.

Target or Niche Marketing

Richard Weylman says it best in his book, *Opening Closed Doors*. "Target or Niche marketing is about dividing the marketplace into definable segments or groups of people." In other words, a target or niche market is a definable segment or group of people who network and communicate with one another. In your local bookstore you will find many books on creating niche markets, bulls-eye marketing and so forth. All of them have a different approach when it comes to marketing. The one thing that all the books agree on,

"A key question to ask in your own business is how to get your market to become the marketers for your product or service."

however, is that there is power in segmenting and there is power in focus. Let me sum up this concept with this adage: "Smaller the niche, bigger the dollar."

To prove my point, let me ask you a question. Who makes more money, the dentist or the orthodontist? Who does the marketing for the orthodontist? That is right, the dentist as well as the orthodontist. A key question to ask in your own business is how to get your market to become the marketers for your product or service. I believe target or niche marketing is the key.

The first step in identifying your target or niche markets is to take an in-depth look at who is already buying from you. Look closely at who your customers have been for the last few years and start looking for some similarities. Do not focus on the demographics of your customers, look for common characteristics such as how they network and how they communicate. I believe that demographics point you in the general direction of your market but they are not as focused as networking and communication similarities.

If you are trying to increase your piece of the market pie, while improving your margins, then you must become a target or niche marketer. Too many sales professionals spend their time prospecting and selling all over the marketplace. They never take the time to develop a specialty. Of course I am not suggesting that you should work in just one vertical market segment. I am saying that you should take the time to break down your markets into small niches or segments and focus your marketing and selling efforts against these segments. You should only have as many niches or market segments as you can handle. By handle, I mean that you can develop to a point that you become an expert. The more you define your market and specialize within that market, the more productive you will be–and the bigger the premium you can demand for your expertise. Let me illustrate.

My company specializes in the sales training and personal productivity business. Our role is to help our clients become the preferred providers of what they sell. Our marketing is primarily word-of-mouth or advocacy. However, we have created a number of strategies based on the target market strategy. Most businesses believe that they are special and unique, and that their needs are different than the needs of other companies. We operate on the premise that companies, given the choice, would rather deal with specialists in their business than generalists. If you think about it for a minute, I am sure you would also choose a specialist within your field to help resolve issues you might be having, rather than a service provider you consider to be a generalist.

One of the many lucrative market segments in the sales training business in which we wanted to develop some expertise was the insurance industry. So what did we do? We joined their trade associations, and we attended their conferences and conventions. We signed up to receive their newsletters and industry publications, and we read their trade journals. We began to understand their politics, their issues, and their stresses. We wanted to know everything we could about the insurance industry. Our marketing materials were then customized to that industry. We even developed an industry-specific web site. Today, we do understand their issues, and we can promote ourselves as experts in their field. We write articles for their industry, we continue to attend their conferences, and we exhibit at their trade shows. Other clients and potential clients also want us to become specialists in their businesses. Are we really experts in the insurance industry? Probably not. But we do know more about their industry than our competitors and therefore we are perceived and considered to be specialists in the insurance industry.

Another example is the real estate industry, in which we are also perceived to be experts. Again we have done the same things. We belong to their associations, and we attend their conferences and conventions. We receive their newsletters and industry publications, we read their trade journals, and we understand their politics, their issues, and their stresses. The real estate industry perceives us to be experts in their business. Are we really experts in their industry? Again, probably not, but we know more about the real estate industry than most

"The key, however, is to become an expert within that industry. To do that, we direct our marketing materials specifically towards each vertical or target market and we address the needs of each of those markets."

of our competitors, and therefore we are considered specialists or experts by the industry. The net result is that our target marketing has been successful.

If you were to investigate the transportation industry, the printing industry, the computer industry, or the financial services industry, it would be the same story over and over again. We work in a myriad of industries because our products and services are beneficial to entrepreneurial and sales organizations regardless of their particular industry. The key, however, is to become an expert within that industry. To do that, we direct our marketing materials specifically towards each vertical or target market and we address the needs of each of those markets. We have created all of these niche markets. We have also created a competitive advantage because our clients would much rather work with specialists than with generalists.

Vertical Expansion
Once you have created expertise in a particular industry, you can expand your marketing efforts vertically. Let us take the oil and gas industry as an example. We identified a specific need that was relevant to that industry, and we customized our marketing materials, our workbooks, and our teaching examples to reflect the nuances of that industry. Of course we did everything else in addition to developing our expertise in oil and gas matters. We attended their association meetings, we attended their conferences, and we read their journals and

newsletters. As a consequence, we became experts in their field. Once we developed this expertise, we asked ourselves how we could leverage our knowledge to capitalize on our expertise. The answer was logical. Go vertical and work with everyone in the oil and gas food chain.

So that is what we did.

Now we work with the oil producers, the transport companies, and even the oil and gas marketing companies. We work with the engineers and the executives. We work with everyone in the corporate food chain. Once you have defined a niche, work that target market as deep and as wide as you possibly can. You do this because companies in your niche markets will have two things in common. They network and they communicate with each other. Since we know that word of mouth advertising or advocacy is the best form of advertising, we count on these recommendations and on the inner network and communication to help develop our business further within the target market. And, of course, it works.

Remember that birds of a feather flock together. Attorneys hang out with other attorneys. Doctors hang out with other doctors. Truck drivers hang out with other truck drivers. Presidents of companies hang out with presidents of other companies. Moms hang out with other moms. As a speaker and author guess who I hang out with? Other writers and speakers. The reason I hang out with them is that I have something in common with them. They speak my language. So if you were to sell to me and you were a specialist in my industry, word would get around quickly. I would gladly refer you to my colleagues. Suppose that you sell insurance; you call me up on the telephone, introduce yourself and say something like: "Mr. Vickers, my name is John. I was referred to you by Stephen Covey. I specialize in the speaking industry. I have discovered that your needs are different than others." [Are they really? No, but I think they are, so now he has my attention.] "I would like to show you how I have satisfied those needs for other speakers and authors like Stephen." Guess what? He is in with that approach.

In competitive situations we will win the majority of the business over our competitors if we are perceived as experts and they appear as generalists or if they do not specialize at all within the market segment. If you were going to spend $10,000 on a product or service, would you buy it from a company that you perceived to be an expert in that field, or would you be happy enough to buy it from a company that simply sold products in all markets? The answer is obvious. The problem with most sales organizations today is that they try to be all things to all people. They are perceived as jack-of-all-trades, masters of none. The rule of thumb is simple. You can have as many vertical or niche markets as you want, but be sure to break them down into definable segments and develop expertise in each one.

Finding Your Target Market

There are many places you can go when it comes to defining your market segments. You can start by looking at your current customer base. Get a list of your customers and break them down according to the following questions:

1. What type of business are they in?
2. What type of occupation are they in?
3. What type of profession are they in?
4. What do they do when they are not working?
5. Where and when do they meet to discuss issues pertinent to their industry?
6. What do they read?
7. Who are their suppliers?
8. Where do they advertise?

If you look closely you might see vertical market patterns starting to emerge. You might find that you actually have several customers within a certain defined market segment already. Or you might notice how little they have in common demographically. Once you have identified who is on your customer list, you can easily identify who is not on it, but who is still within the same industry or business chain. This then becomes your target market.

If you are just starting a new territory or perhaps just starting your own business, you should choose which markets will become your focus if you want to increase your chance of success. For example, I know a sales professional who sells business insurance. He also loves to ski. He decided that he wanted to develop a practice that would allow him to perform his work duties and at the same time give him an opportunity to ski. So he developed a market that focused on ski resorts. He attended their trade shows and their conventions. He read their magazines and their newsletters. He learned everything that his clients need to know to conduct their business, making himself an expert in what they do. He now also markets to the ski product manufacturers and to the distribution companies. He also services many professional athletes in the sport of skiing. He has become successful in his practice because he chose to focus his efforts, and he was smart enough to specialize in and build his practice around what he loves to do. Consequently, his work has become his play. He sells a basic commodity product or service, but has become the insurance agent to the winter sports industry because of his self-proclaimed specialty. And his compensation reflects his specialization. He becomes preferred in his market by focusing his efforts and becoming an expert to a specialized market.

Let me give you another example of a successful sales professional. Let us call her Jennifer. Jennifer is also in the insurance industry. Jennifer has two small children and had a difficult time balancing work and family She felt guilty going to work days and evenings and not spending time with her children. As Jennifer thought about what vertical or niche market she could go after, she came up with this idea. As a mother, she understands the stress of other mothers. She also understands the needs, wants, and concerns that mothers have about their children. So Jennifer created a special education program for mothers concerned about college education funds for their children.

At least twice a week Jennifer gets a member of her target market (a mom with children) to hold a morning information seminar on college education funds for children. She brings the donuts, the babysitter, and her two children. The other moms love it, word-of-mouth has spread quickly and now Jennifer makes more money than she did when she worked fulltime. Jennifer has become a "college education specialist." Her products and services have remained the same and are not necessarily unique (universal life insurance and mutual funds). The secret to Jennifer's success, however, is that she developed a market where her prospects network and communicate with one other. She offered knowledge-based Distinctive Value by addressing the needs of other mothers, both in the products she offered and the way in which she offered them. As a result, she became preferred in her market.

Here is one more example. After one of my seminars, a woman named Carol came up to speak to me. She was frustrated with her career and asked for advice. She sold fine furniture as part of her interior decorating business, and was having difficulty getting established in a highly competitive marketplace. I asked her about her background. "I worked as a manager in a dental office for about eight years," Carol told me. Bingo! There was the key. "All right," I asked her, "do you know how to gain access to dentists better than any of your competitors?" "I guess so," she responded. "Now who understands the stress that dentists go through better than the manager of the dentist's office? And who does the buying for the dentist? Mrs. Dentist, I would assume. Do you know how to gain access to Mrs. Dentist?" "Yes, I do," she responded. "Who do you think Mrs. Dentist hangs out with? Other Mrs. Dentists." So now Carol specializes in selling fine furniture and interior decorating services to the dental profession. In most cases she is getting full margins for her services because she is regarded as a specialist in the dental industry.

Once you define your markets, there are plenty of tools that you can use to uncover potential clients or customers within those markets. There are many bureaus and list brokers that will help you fine tune your market and focus on your selected industry segments. Once you have identified those segments, work them deep and work them wide. Find the common relationships that will provide a basis upon which you can build your business.

Networking

Let us take a moment and focus on a forgotten skill that can produce significant return on your marketing investment. It is also part of the identification or marketing strategy we discussed earlier. I am talking about networking. Networking is a very misunderstood concept. I have seen very few sales professionals who network effectively. Most sales people think networking means simply talking to your friends about other people you can contact. But successful networking means so much more.

Here are some simple steps that you can take to build a successful network:

Step 1. Make a list of everyone you know who trusts you. These people might be found in your business and personal network. They may be people you work with, people you went to school with, or people from clubs, industry associations, and church or community associations. Do not leave anyone out.

Step 2. From this list, make another list of the people you will get together with in the next thirty days. Contact these people and ask them to introduce you to someone you do not currently know, who they feel might benefit from your products or services. Do not be shy about leveraging your contacts to meet new people, especially those whom you are interested in contacting. Remember the rule of six degrees of separation. There is never more than six relationships between you and anyone you are trying to meet.

Step 3. Create your own breakfast club. Identify the people in your personal network who share similar clients to yours and who could help you gain access to prospects within your key niche markets. Then put together a weekly, biweekly, or monthly breakfast club where you get together to meet and discuss ways to mutually benefit each other. I suggest you get as many people as possible together who share common market segments.

Your Introduction

As you expand your network, you will need to develop a powerful self-introduction. I am sure you will agree that first impressions are everything. One of the purposes of this book is to help you set yourself apart from the competition. To do so, you have to focus on your individuality and find ways to differentiate yourself. A powerful self-introduction will go a long way to helping you achieve that.

The most important thing you can do in formulating a powerful introduction is to first define the benefits of what you do rather than simply describing what you do. For example, let us say that I sell insurance. You meet me at the local watering hole and during the course of our conversation you ask me what I do for a living. I reply, "I sell insurance." Do you need any more information? Do you feel like introducing me to all of your friends? Do you get an overwhelming urge to invite me home for dinner and develop a relationship with me? I don't think so. Let's face it, there is nothing wrong with selling insurance, it is just that you have been there and done that! Saying you sell insurance does not create excitement nor does it create interest.

A number of years ago I was in a golf tournament. During the course of the tournament I struck up a conversation with a professional looking gentleman whom I had not met before. The initial conversation was polite and then I asked him what he did for a living. He replied, "I am a golf fund specialist." That caught my curiosity and I replied, "What do you mean a golf fund specialist?" "Well," he said, "I help executives enjoy the game of Golf today and well into their retirement." "How do you do that?" I asked. He then stated, "I would love to show you how I do it. If you give me your business card I will be happy to give you a call and perhaps we can continue this conversation over coffee."

Am I interested in meeting with this person? Absolutely. Guess what he does for a living? He sells insurance! The products he sells are financial products, but the benefit of what he sells is financial security. His marketing target is the business professional who golfs. The market has thousands of insurance agents and financial planners, but how many "golf fund specialists" do you know? It is not what you do that counts, but the benefit of what you do.

Let us recap for a moment. You have identified your target or niche markets either through your own network or with the help of others. You have armed yourself with a new title and introduction that will stimulate interest. Now you need to gain access to your selected markets. Here are some steps you can take to gain access.

Step One: Pre-call research

The reason why pre-call research is important to the access process is because people today do not have time to meet with a salesperson they know nothing about. Why? No trust. They also do not want to waste their time with a sales professional who does not know anything about their business.

To gain a prospect's trust you should gain an understanding of their business and the issues that limit them from meeting or exceeding their goals and targets. You can do this by searching out company information from the internet and their web sites, accessing annual reports, looking them up in trade journals or associations, reading articles about them and talking to their competitors. You should also talk to anyone in your own network who may know of them or their business.

Step Two: Referrals

Getting referrals is an important part of the access strategy for three reasons: A referral generates 80 percent more results than a cold call; approximately 70 percent of all jobs are found through referrals; and most people you meet have at least 250 contacts.

Networking is a powerful strategy because people buy from people they trust. They are much more likely to talk to you and allow you access to their world if you come with a recommendation or introduction from one of their friends.

To be effective at gaining access to a prospective client, however, make sure that the person who gave you the reference contacts them first to tell them that you will be calling. This is a form of giving permission, and it will put the prospective client at ease when you do in fact call. They will be expecting you and will not be surprised by your contact.

Secondly, if at all possible, try to arrange a personal introduction to a prospective client through your contact. The purpose of this is to create a comfort level with the prospective client - you want them to feel that you are someone they can trust. This is facilitated by your common contact. In addition, you can use the meeting to learn more about the person's business and to discover the key challenges that prevent them from achieving their goals. Nothing is more powerful in networking than the personal introduction. If it is at all possible, make the personal introduction happen. It is the most effective way to build a new relationship with a prospective client.

Step Three: The knowledge-based Distinctive Value drip strategy

The purpose of this strategy, as I discussed earlier, is to show your value to your market rather than simply telling them how much value you can bring them. The key to making your information drip strategy successful is to not send prospective clients any information about your products or services. Operate on the premise that they do not care. Trust that they will ask you for information about your business when they need it. Send them tiny pieces of information that you know will help them resolve personal and professional stress and help them become more productive.

For illustration purposes, let us suppose that you are a stock broker. You have identified two niche markets or segments that you want to pursue: entrepreneurs and company presidents. You have also identified their primary professional challenge: how to grow their companies profitably.

One way that you might entice them with your Distinctive Value is to send them a "Business Tip of the Week" filled with ideas about how to grow profitability. Notice that this topic has nothing to do with your products and services but everything to do

"When the information has everything to do with their business or their challenges then the information becomes useful and valuable."

with their business. That is the key. If it has anything to do with your business, it will come across as commercial or corporate hype. When the information has everything to do with their business or their challenges then the information becomes useful and valuable. You are demonstrating to your prospect that you care more about their business than your own.

Your customers and prospects are bombarded with information and they have no time to read and assimilate what they already have. Make the information that you send to them valuable. It becomes valuable when it relates to their core competency and when it helps them remove personal or professional stress. Sending such information will make you a valuable resource to your prospect. Remember that knowledge-based Distinctive Value is the ultimate currency.

The key to having the Distinctive Value Drip Strategy work is effective follow-up. I suggest that you follow-up with new prospects after six weeks of dripping. Why six weeks? Based on my experience, if you send information weekly, it takes about three to four weeks before the prospect starts to notice you. By then you will only have aroused their curiosity. By the sixth week their curiosity should be fully engaged. Then you make your follow-up call to determine whether you are providing the prospect with some value-added information or whether you are simply being a nuisance. They will always let you know the truth.

If they respond positively, keep in mind that they are beginning to trust you. Depending upon the level of their positive response, it might be a good time to ask for an opportunity to meet them in order to show them some other innovative ideas that you feel can help them grow their business, increase their market-share, and save them money.

If they respond with a negative statement of interest in the information that you have been sending, then move on. If the person sees no value in the valuable ideas that others enjoy getting, then the time that you spend working with them will not likely be very productive.

If the client calls you with a positive response before your scheduled follow-up, congratulations, you have just become the EXPERT! They called you because you have stirred their curiosity with the information that you have been providing them.

The Distinctive Value Drip Strategy is designed to help build relationships of trust. Rather than cold calling and asking for business, like most of your competitors, you will come from a place of contribution–rather than being perceived as wanting something from them.

The process of sharing value with prospective customers enables you to touch hundreds and thousands of qualified buyers on a regular basis, even if you do not have time to sell to them. One of the common problems with cold calling is that you spend a lot of time doing it, but when you get some opportunities to work with, you have to stop cold calling because your plate is full. Once you have sold the existing opportunities, you have to start the process all over again. Your sales production line is stop-start and is filled with hills and valleys. The drip strategy will keep your prospect funnel full. If you ever run out of opportunities, you can simply go to the database and call some new prospects to whom you have been dripping information. They will be well aware of you because you will have been in touch with them regularly.

You will often get calls from people because they are dissatisfied with a supplier and they have just received your tip that morning. Remember that your competitors are showing up only when they want something. You show up every week and you are contributing valuable information that helps them remove professional or personal stress. The benefit of this strategy is that you are able to build relationships of trust more quickly. This will accelerate the buying cycle. Gaining access and building relationships of trust with your market is a process.

The Briefing

It is now time to go to the briefing stage of the selling process. There are five basic objectives in the briefing stage:

Step 1. Build trust.
Step 2. Identify their personal and
professional challenges.

Step 3. Perform a needs analysis and
identify dissatisfaction factors.

Step 4. Stir their interest.

Step 5. Create an impending event.

Here is one example of how you might conduct your briefings:

"Thank you again for the time. Just a quick time check, I asked for twenty minutes. Is that still okay with you? In order to stay focused and make the best use of our time, I have prepared a number of questions for you that with your permission I would like to ask."

Prospect: "Sure, go ahead."

Now you can start with some questions that are not too intrusive but will give you valuable information. Remember, you are looking for areas in which they are dissatisfied. I call them "dissatisfiers". Your questions should help you identify their challenges and needs, and discover how they conduct their business and determine their customer service expectations.

There are basically two types of questions you should ask: primary and secondary. The secondary questions are those questions that come from the briefing itself, as well as from any conversations that you have with a client. They are the follow-up questions that you ask when you get on a topic of interest to the client. They always spring from the primary questions. Primary questions are those that you determine in advance.

Do not wing the primary questions! If you do, you will leave the briefing and forget to ask something that is critical to the sales process. Here is what I do. I develop an inventory of all the primary questions I want to ask. I type them out and I put an asterix beside the questions that are most important to me. I like to show up at my first meeting with the client carrying a file folder that has their name typed on a label. It sends an important message to the potential client–it shows them that you take care of the details. I have my list of primary questions inside the folder and I am not afraid to bring this out during the meeting and refer to it while asking questions. Again, it shows preparation and organization and can only be considered positive.

The questions that you ask will differ depending on your industry. However, I can give you some basic question categories to help you get started. You will notice that many of the questions are closed-ended; that is they require either a "yes" or a "no" for an answer. For years sales trainers have taught that we should only ask open-ended questions. But I like to create a mix of questions, with both open and closed ones. Closed questions can often be useful in getting your client to follow a logic map leading them to a conclusion that you desire–a recognition of the fact that they need your services! The technique lies in structuring your questions in such a way that they give you pertinent information and at the same time lead the client and you to the next logical question in the sequence, drawing you both closer to the desired conclusion. Imagine a lawyer questioning the witness on the stand. The lawyer's questions are focused, and they always keep the lawyer in control. Lawyers ask their questions in a logical order to uncover important information and lead the witness to the conclusion that the questioning lawyer desires. This should be your goal as well.

The following are some categories that you should consider including in your portfolio of primary questions. Obviously, they can be changed to better match your industry or the selected clients you are seeking. But they should provide you with a good place to start.

Technology Questions

The goal in this category is to determine your prospect's level of technological sophistication. Try to determine if they are a company that readily adapts to new changes in technology. Are they early adopters or are they the last ones to jump on board? Determine their priorities regarding technology. Are they on the web? Do they effectively use the Internet in their business either as a marketing tool or to enhance product supply? Do they have the latest computers or equipment in their office? What is their long-term technology strategy, if any?

Here are some examples of questions that you might consider using:

- Does technology give your company a competitive advantage? If so, how?

- How committed is your company to using technology for competitive advantage?

- What resources has your company committed to technology?

When new technology comes into the marketplace, some companies rush out to have the latest in the market, some companies prefer to wait and see if the technology is going to stay around and some companies are the last ones to join the band wagon. Where does your company fit in?

- How has technology helped or hurt your business in the past?

- How does your company use technology in its business processes?

- How have your competitors used technology to gain an advantage over your company?

Sizing Questions

The goal of using sizing questions is to skillfully determine how big a client they could be, without being too obvious. You have to be a little tricky on this one. Try not to get specific too quickly, but rather ask questions that are geared towards determining whether or not you can meet their needs. Try asking questions that will give you an idea of the total amount of business that you could expect someday from them, should they be inclined to use your services or products.

Here are some examples of questions that you might ask:

- Do you take advantage of volume discounts as a purchasing priority?

- Who does your purchasing, and what is their position in the company? (This will tell you how much of a priority they place on purchasing.)

If, for example, you are selling telecommunication equipment and you are trying to determine how many telephones they might need, you could ask a question like:

- How many employees work in this building? You could then make an educated guess as to how many telephones they would need.

Or, if you were selling photocopiers, you could ask:

- How many copies do you produce a year?

Or perhaps you could ask questions like:

- Last year, what was your total budget for widgets?

The idea is to determine how much business there is, and what your share of it might be.

Timing

Try to establish their timeframes and urgency level with questions such as these:

- Do you use a just-in-time delivery system?

- How do you conduct your business?

- Do you use any traditional project planning programs?

- What is critical in your business that drives timing, and what is not?

- What is a comfortable inventory load?

- How far in advance do you plan your purchases?

Some other questions that you might ask include:

- If you were to find a solution that met your needs exactly, how soon would you be implementing it?

- Is this something that is planned for this year's budget or for next year's?

- In which quarter would you ideally like to have it implemented?

- Could you tell me about the decision-making process in your business from a timing point of view?

- How much of a priority is this?

Learning about their timing priorities will help you classify them as a prospect, and it will help you determine how you should prioritize them in your business.

Competition Questions

The purpose of this category is to gain an understanding of who you are competing against so that you can develop a game plan. Ask questions that will help you determine how many suppliers they are currently using that compete with your products or services. What do they like most about their current supplier? Why did they leave the last one? How much of the market pie do they give each supplier?

Some other questions that you might ask include:

- Do you currently have a supplier or suppliers for this service?

- What do you like most about your current supplier?

- What do you like least?

- Who were you using before your current supplier?

- Why did you change?

Again, try to find out information that you can use to shape your products or services to fit your prospect's needs and to help prevent you from making any mistakes that their past suppliers might have made.

Budget Questions

The purpose of this category is to get an idea of budgets, timing, and their decision-making process as it relates to money. This is where you should ask questions about their buying process, and who is involved in their decision-making.

Some questions that you might ask include:

- How much do you spend on similar products or services on an annual basis?

- Do you have plans to expand your budgets at any time in the future?

- Do you believe you are spending enough on the products or services that you offer?

You might also ask:

- Has a budget been set for this product or service?

- What is your budget this year?

- When are your budgets fixed during the calendar year?

- Does your budget regularly increase on an annual basis, or is your business in a cost-cutting mode?

- Are you looking for cost savings in this area?

- If it could help you generate more revenues or profits, would you be willing to spend more?

- Besides yourself, who else is responsible for the decision to spend in this area?

Try to get a feel as to whether or not this business is in an expansive climate or a shrinking climate. This will enable you to gear your presentation either towards growth, or savings, or both.

Expectations Questions

Questions in this category are designed to enable you to get a clear understanding of what they expect from a vendor. Have them paint a picture of what the perfect vendor would look like and how they expect problems to be solved.

Some questions that you might ask include:

- If you could wave a magic wand and create the perfect vendor, what would they look like?

- What problems have you experienced with vendors in the past?

- What do you like most (or least) about the vendors you currently use?

- What are your expectations on quality, service, pricing, and terms?

Coming out of this area of questioning, you want to feel comfortable about what issues you must avoid to keep their business, and what areas or issues will help you win them away from their current suppliers.

Customer Service Questions

In this category, you want to look for ways to exceed their expectations by delivering "wow" customer service. Have them identify two or three companies that give them wow customer service today. My guess is they will be hard pressed to come up with answers in their own supplier group. But if they can identify them, ask them specifically what they like about the service offered and why they consider it "wow" customer service.

Some other questions that you might ask are:

- Does your company put a value on great customer service?

- What does your company consider to be "good" customer service?

- What do your customers think of your service?

- Do you routinely question your customers or hand out surveys to them to determine how happy they are with you?

- How would you define "bad" customer service?

- Can you give me an example of a supplier that practices good (or bad) customer service?

If you can find out what they believe to be good customer service, and find out how often they have experienced it, you will be better able to assess their expectations and then determine whether or not it is within your capability to exceed those expectations.

Personal Questions

Do not underestimate the importance of this category of questioning. In many business relationships the bottom line is that if they like you, they will do business with you. And the best way to have them like you is to build a personal relationship with them. Get to know what your prospect enjoys doing with his or her personal time. This can be the most rewarding of all the question categories.

Whenever I get to the door and I am about to shake hands and say goodbye, I usually look them in the eye and say, "When you are not working ten hours a day, what do you do for fun?" This can be one of the most important questions in the whole process. Their response will give you some clues on what makes them tick, what their passions are, and how you can help them get closer to the activities they really enjoy.

Each time that you have an opportunity to visit the prospect, try to find out something personal about him or her. Remember that every great sales presentation is filled with questions. Questions are what guide your prospect or customer through the buying process. Questions about their personal life are also important, for they will help you build the relationship. Relationship will be the reason why your clients will want to do business with you, or not. Do not underestimate this area.

General Questions

Here are some other general questions that you could integrate into your briefings to develop a greater understanding of your potential with a particular client.

- What is your main objective as it relates to this product or service?

Once you gain an understanding of your prospect's goals, you can then customize your presentation or proposal to directly reflect their needs.

- How do you plan to achieve that objective?

This one is important. The prospect or client might have already decided to have you and your company as part of the solution. Listen carefully to the response – the prospect himself might just close the deal.

- What are some of the challenges that prevent you from achieving your objective?

Some of the challenges might or might not be directly related to your product or service. By asking this question you can potentially win big brownie points if you can solve some of their issues.

- How are you currently handling this challenge?

This will give you some idea about the priority of this challenge and about their time frame for solving it.

- Is there anyone standing in the way of solving this challenge?

This will help you identify the antagonists to the solution.

- Besides yourself, who else would like to see a solution to this challenge?

This will help you identify supporters.

- What would be the value to your company of a solution to the challenge or problem?

Here you can expect to get a better understanding of their sense of your potential worth to them.

- What would be the cost to the company if things remained the same?

With this question you might find out whether they are motivated more by fear or by opportunity.

- Are there any alternatives that you have considered?

This will help you identify who your competitors might be.

- How would you personally benefit from solving this challenge?

Remember people buy first for personal reasons and then justify their purchases with business rationale. They might be reluctant to answer this one but try to pursue it.

- How would others in your organization benefit from a solution?

This will help you create justification for their purchase of your product or service.

- How do you see that I can help?

Pay attention to this one. You might find by listening to the answer that the deal is already closed for you. If not, follow up with questions to identify why they are hesitant.

- What questions have I not asked that I should ask?

This will help you identify any unresolved issues.

- In your mind, what is the next step?

This is where the prospect or customer will tell you what is necessary to move the deal ahead.

- If we were to find a solution that met your needs exactly, how soon would you be prepared to execute?

Obviously, this will let you know how serious they are or could be.

- What is your time frame on delivery?

This question will give you some idea as to what their priority is for your product or service.

- When would be a good time for me to get back to you with some recommended solutions?

Never leave the briefing without having a follow-up schedule.

Follow up

An important part of the sales process is what you do after the briefing part. Often business is won or lost by what you do or fail to do following a sales call. When you are in the briefing, and you begin asking really good questions that get your prospects talking, resist the urge to solve their problems right there and then. Even if the prospect brings up an issue that you know you can provide a sure-fire solution for, hold off from providing the solution. Remember that if you do provide the solution, you stop the prospect from talking and you might lose the opportunity to uncover even greater information that might prove critical to you in making the sale. Just take notes and listen.

When the briefing is up, end your meeting by saying something like, "My time is up; thank you for giving me some of your time today. There were several issues that you raised that I don't think I can be any help with. On the other hand you identified several issues that I believe I can help you with, and I believe I may have some solutions that you will be delighted with. I would like to go back to my office and do some homework. Let's schedule a follow-up where I can report back to you on some possible solutions." You then schedule your follow-up meeting and head for the door.

As you get to the door, shake their hand and then ask this question: "When you are not working ten hours a day, what do you do for fun?" This will help you identify some of their personal interests in a non-threatening way. I have used the information from their response to this one question to close many transactions.

When you get back to the office, research solutions to their questions and prepare for the follow-up presentations. Incorporate something into your follow-up program that involves their personal interests if at all possible. Preferred providers execute their follow-up very quickly Responding quickly keeps the subject and you fresh in the mind of the prospect. You have invested time gaining momentum for your product or service and now is the time to act. Do it fast.

Value-Added Strategy

As you prepare for your follow-up, make sure you present solutions based on the buying style of the person that you are working with. This part of the process relies upon your experience. The solutions that you are going to bring to the table, the quality of your product or service, and the ideas that you generate are all up to you. But be creative, and try to think out of the box. That is where your competitors are not thinking.

"In a competitive marketplace, often the difference between success and failure is the perceived value of the value-added services that you can offer."

As part of your follow-up and recommendations, I suggest that you include a detailed list of value-added services that you can offer. This will help you in the confirmation part of your process. In a competitive marketplace, often the difference between success and failure is the perceived value of the value-added services that you can offer.

The value-added strategy is designed to give you a competitive advantage by demonstrating to the buyer that they will get more value for their dollar by working with you than by working with your competitor. Create an inventory of all the value-added services that your company can provide. Include everything that you can deliver: training, 24 by 7 technical support, location, warehousing, and state of the art technology.

Here are four categories of value-added strategies to help get you started with your list:

Support value
Identify your training and education programs, testing and quality control, safety programs, research and development abilities, special projects expertise, and anything that you think you could do to meet your client's needs.

Consulting value
Here you could identify any studies, database development, technical or service support, product or

service design, computer or technology systems, quality management services, or any other educational services that you could provide to a client, – whether you are able to do it yourself or whether you could hire someone to work with you and provide the client with the services.

Promotional value

Think of anything that you could do to help promote and market your client's business. This list could include samples or trials, cooperative advertising, sales materials, brochures or literature, seminars, conventions, trade-shows, business development, referrals, leads, and networking.

Emotional value

This area will be unique to each account. These are ideas that you create on an individual basis. They could include things such as favors, executive briefings, preparing presentations for your client to deliver, special projects, or personal projects.

Once you have identified your value-added services, you can then quantify them. This means that you must attach a price or value to them. This is where it can get a little tricky. Do your best to evaluate the costs of those services, and then, depending on how much you need to leverage them to get the deal you want, assess a price or value to give to the prospect. Do not worry if you do not have it right. You will know quickly from their reaction if your assessment is out-of-line.

Whenever I ask my audiences how much they spend on value-added services, I usually get a blank stare. That is because they do not know the value of the specific services they usually purchase. Going through the process of attaching a specific value is important because it will enable you to define for your potential client the real worth of what you are offering. This is something your competitors have likely not done.

Now that you have identified and quantified your value-added services, you must now sell them. There are four areas in which you have an opportunity to sell them:

1. The Sales call

The first area is the sales call itself. Whenever you are on a sales call, look for ways to bring out the value of some of your services. Perhaps you are talking to a client about their consulting needs and you happen to drop the little known fact that your company spends 10 percent of its revenues on research and development. Your client or prospect might respond with interest in a part of your business of which they were not aware.

2. Briefings and presentations

The second opportunity you have to sell your value-added services is when you are conducting your briefings or presentations. Make sure that you link the value-added service to a direct benefit for the prospect or customer. Do not make it the focus of your presentation though. Stay focused on your sales strategy.

3. Sales negotiations

A third opportunity is during sales negotiations. When you are in a negotiation with a prospect or client always identify your value-added services and quantify their value in actual dollars. Use quiet moments to raise your value-added services and test your client's reaction to them. If they show interest, pursue the line of questioning that will bring them to understand they need such services.

4. Competitive situations

Last but not least are competitive situations. This is one of my favorites. I use this strategy in several ways. One of the ways I use it is during the annual business review. I call the client and request a meeting for an annual business review. I mention that I will be looking for feedback on how we can improve our level of service and create more real value during the upcoming year.

During the meeting I might say something like this: "Mr. Client, during this last year you were one of our most valued clients. Here are the products and services that we provided to you. You will notice that your total purchase with our company was approximately $1 million. You should be aware of the extra value that we provided. We spent $150,000 or 15 percent of your purchases on these additional services, and we did not charge you for them. We were happy to provide them last year at no charge and we will be happy to provide them again this year, again at no charge. I thought you should be aware of them."

By letting them know that you provided these additional services, you have built an additional 15 percent value into your price structure. This extra 15 percent will help you the next time your competitor comes in and tries to undermine your price by 5 or 10 percent. You have already established the fact that you are providing an additional 15 percent in value-added services, so your client will be less likely to react positively to the price competition.

The other way I use this strategy in competitive situations is to itemize the value-added services on the invoice. I note the price or value of the value-added service, and then I put a "no charge" in the extended portion of the invoice. These are usually normal costs of doing business. It is not a problem if you give them away for free, but make sure that you let the client know their worth. Remember, if you do not communicate your value, you lose your value.

Confirming the business

The sales books are filled with great closes. We could spend countless hours learning all of the great closes that are available. But I do not believe there is a moment in time where it all boils down to "the close." I believe the close is really the conclusion of a process.

If you have done your homework, asked all of the right questions, taken the time to identify their needs, and gained a good understanding of their issues and key challenges, then the close is simply the next natural

"Remember, if you do not communicate your value, you lose your value."

step in the process. If you have done it right, your prospective client will feel this way also.

The most effective close that I know is simply this: After you have recapped, asked great questions and done your homework, work out several solutions that make sense. Remember to include a low-cost solution, a middle of the road solution, and a money is no object solution. Present them to your client and say, "Based on all of the information you have given me and based on our discussions, these three solutions make the most sense to me. Which one makes the most sense to you?"

By offering a selection of options that make sense, you give the buyer an opportunity to select a solution that works best for them. If it makes sense-then it makes sense; it is enough. You do not need any fancy words or techniques to close the deal. It will happen anyway or it won't-for reasons that you cannot control. If your solutions make sense, however, and are based on the information you learned during the briefing, and are coupled with something of personal interest for your client, then chances are you will close the deal most of the time. Your job is to worry about the process, not the result. Take care of the process, and the results will take care of themselves.

The Relationship Formula

The first two sections of "Becoming Preferred" covered creating distinctive value and the sales process. This section covers the fundamentals of the business relationship.

In my seminars and workshops, I routinely ask my audience to imagine that I have assembled the finest sales professionals in their company all in one room. I then inform them that I am going to write a newsletter that will influence thousands of their potential customers, and I want to include information about them and their company. I invite them to respond to the following question: "Why should your potential customers do business with you?"

I get answers like "We are price competitive," or "We have been around the longest," or "We have 24 by 7 customer service," or "We offer next day delivery service," or "We have the biggest selection," or "We guarantee the lowest prices" and so on. I then ask my audience to imagine for a moment that they are their competitors. Again I ask the question, "Why should your potential customers do business with you?" The responses are almost identical to those given the first time I ask the question.

"If you accept the fact that you and your company created the commodity monster, I can show you and your company how to destroy it."

Finally, I ask my audience to go into the mindset of the customer. Taking away all of the hype and clichés, is there really a difference that counts to the customer in all of the different products and services that are offered? More often than not, the answer is "no". The products look the same, the services look the same, and the salespeople look the same. This is not a recipe for success.

If a bag of rice and a bag of rice and a bag of rice all look the same, how much do I want to pay for it? You guessed it. The lowest price possible. Your product or service, then, becomes perceived as a commodity. Now who created that monster? The fact is that *we* did, the salespeople, the marketing department – everyone involved in the process. I understand that this is not a popular perspective. It would be much easier to blame it on our competitors or our customers or someone else, anyone else, for creating the current business climate. If you insist on blaming others, however, you become a victim of the marketplace, and you are left powerless to change it. If, on the other hand, you take responsibility for creating your business problems, then I can offer some help. If you accept the fact that you and your company created the commodity monster, I can show you and your company how to destroy it.

Relationship Formula

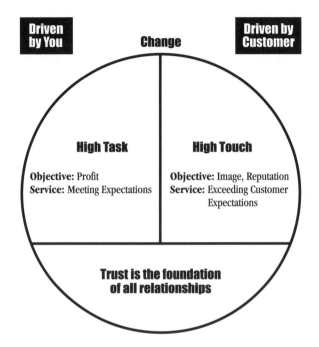

Driven by You

Change

Driven by Customer

High Task

Objective: Profit
Service: Meeting Expectations

High Touch

Objective: Image, Reputation
Service: Exceeding Customer Expectations

Trust is the foundation of all relationships

Trust is the foundation of all relationships. Of course it is possible to have a business relationship without trust. However, you will always lose to the relationship where trust exists. The role of the sales professional is to build relationships of trust with customers. This trust is built over time. There are, however, strategies and tactics that will enable you to build solid relationships of trust more quickly than your normal practice and also more quickly than your competitors.

The relationship formula will show you how to do that. "High Task" is on the left side of the formula. This

is your company's core competency, and it represents
the products and services that your company brings to
the marketplace. This is your expected value. It is
what your company does well and how it makes
money. Making money is one of the primary drivers of
business. Your company is in business to make money.
The goal is to make a profit by offering products and
services that meet the needs of your customers.

"High Touch" is on the right side of the formula.
This part of the formula is driven by the customer.
"High Touch" is about exceeding customers'
expectations. When we significantly exceed our
customers' expectations, we make them go "wow."
When they go "wow," we become preferred. Think for
a moment of two companies that offer "wow" customer
service. (This might be difficult to do.) Do you ever
ask them for a discount? Probably not. One of the
many benefits of becoming preferred in your
marketplace is that you can demand a high profit
margin and your customers are delighted to pay.

I often ask my audiences, "What do you do on the
"High Touch" side of things? What do you do to exceed
customer expectations?" This usually draws a few
blank stares. Then, after a moment of digesting the
question, I get responses like, "We take time to listen to
our customers," or "We do what we say we are going to
do," or "We ensure the quality of our products or
services," or "We take time to understand our clients'

"We must work hard to continually raise the bar and eat our own lunch before the competition does."

needs." The list of clichés goes on and on. All of these things are important and are critical to business success. But the question to ask is, "Do they enable you and your company to significantly exceed customer expectations?" If they are simply meeting our clients' expectations then we should be doing them anyway. These are things that should not be classified as High Touch, but rather should be considered as part of our core competency or High Task offering. High Touch customer care is achieved when we exceed our customers' expectations, not when we simply meet them.

I believe that there is always an opportunity to differentiate ourselves from our competitors through the application of High Touch strategies. But to do so, we have to spend as much time "thinking on the business as we spend thinking in the business." It is especially important to dedicate some time to this process because what is considered High Touch today will become High Task tomorrow. Somebody right now is working to develop High Touch strategies for your business. We must work hard to continually raise the bar and eat our own lunch before the competition does.

I am going to illustrate what I mean by High Touch customer care with a number of stories. It is important that you pay attention to the moral of the stories rather than just their facts. A couple of years ago I was in the office of the president of a major office products company. I was doing my best to generate interest in my products and services. I could tell that I was getting nowhere fast. You know that feeling when you are speaking with someone and you can tell it is going in one ear and out the other.

As I looked around his office, I noticed a variety of sports paraphernalia from an NHL franchise on the wall. I also noticed pictures of his children. I knew from a previous conversation that he had a son about the same age as my son. I mentioned to him that the last game of the NHL season was between his favorite team and my favorite team. I asked him whether he and his son would like to be the guest of my son and I at the hockey game. He readily consented and we made the arrangements.

In my world, it is a common thing to take a client or a potential client to a major sporting event such as a hockey game. It happens all the time. I do it, and my competitors do it. So I do not consider taking a client to a game as significantly exceeding customer expectations or a High Touch strategy, like many people would. Rather, that part is simply business as usual. High Touch differentiation, however, is about to begin.

During the second period of the game, I had the mascot for the local hockey team come up to our seats and have his picture taken with my prospect's son. The little boy had a huge grin on his face and of course so did his dad. At the conclusion of the game, the father thanked me and said that he and his son had a great time. I then surprised him by telling him that the night was not over yet, since I had arranged for him and his son to go into the locker room of his favorite team where I had a hat, stick, and jersey waiting for his son. My boy and I stood in the corner of the dressing room minding our own business, since we were hometown fans and the players from the visiting team were talking to his son. My potential client's son got autographs from all of his favorite players. The little boy was ecstatic. Dad had a grin on his face from ear to ear. Daddy became the little boy's hero. Guess who became daddy's hero?

The moral of this story, and our business lesson, is discovering what we can do to become a hero to the people we serve and how can we make them become a hero to the people they serve. Look for opportunities to become a hero to your customers or clients and create events that make your customers or clients look like heroes to the people they serve.

That is what High Touch is all about. It is about significantly exceeding client expectations. It is about creating "wow" in the minds of your customers. In all of the business books, we see example after example of businesses such as Starbucks, Nordstrom, Federal Express and many others who have become preferred in their marketplace because of the "wow" factor they were able to create. When companies exceed expectations, they become preferred and they enjoy high profit margins as a result.

Let me give you another example of exceeding clients' expectations. Let us suppose that you take clients out for lunch occasionally. Here is what I like to do for my clients. I have divided my city into four areas. I select a restaurant in each of these areas and I go see the manager of each of those restaurants. I tell the manager that I bring very important clients to this restaurant and that I would like a particular table to be my table. I then tell the manager that I would like to set up the following arrangement. A day or two before my lunch appointment, I will call and tell them the name of the client with whom I will be having lunch. I will also tell them my client's favorite drink. When we arrive I would like the host to greet us by name and seat us immediately at our table. I would also like our drinks to arrive shortly afterwards without them being ordered. I then ask that our meal be served as usual. However, I ask that the bill not come to the table following the meal. Instead, I give them my credit card number in advance and ask that they add a 20 percent gratuity to my bill. I pick up the receipt on my next visit or have them mailed to my office.

Now comes the big day. I am with my client; we enter the busy restaurant and are greeted by name and shown immediately to our table. After a minute or so our favorite drinks arrive. Has the client started to

notice something yet? We order our meals and discuss
our business. After lunch and our business discussion,
I glance at my watch and suggest to my client that we
should get him or her back to the office. The client
starts looking for the bill. I simply say, "It's looked after;
thank you for being my guest today."

I can tell you firsthand that this simple practice not only
works; it works well. When my clients ask me about it, I
tell them it is indicative of the kind of service I have
come to expect and the kind of service I offer them. I
also tell them that I believe they should expect similar
service from all of their suppliers. The next time that
they go for lunch with one of my competitors, it will
just be a lunch. They will just have a normal
experience. Their lunch experience with me becomes a
"wow" experience. The next time my client has to
choose to go to lunch with me or with my competitor,
who do you think he or she will choose? More
importantly, the next time they are considering giving
work to me or one of my competitors, who do you
think they will choose? If I have been successful at
demonstrating this same kind of exceptional customer
service in my work, they will choose me. What does
this mean? It means I have become preferred.

The key to significantly exceeding your customer's
expectations is to simply "up-level" your event or
service to make it memorable in the mind of your
client. Attention to detail is everything. It does not
take much to up-level an event. It is about paying

attention, thinking creatively and going the extra mile. It is your responsibility to figure out what your competitors are not doing or are not willing to do, and do it. Trust me on this one, the extra effort will be time and money well spent.

Here is one more example of High Touch service that I recently used in a personal relationship. I think it will further illustrate the point. I took my sweetheart to see the play, Les Miserables. We arrived at the theater. All of the men were in suits and looked sharp. All of the ladies looked beautiful in their evening dresses. We were seated and patiently waiting for the program to start. The orchestra was tuning up their instruments. The anticipation was building and you could feel the excitement in the air. You knew this was going to be a terrific evening. With about five minutes to go before the performance, one of the ushers walked into the theater with some roses and some Belgian chocolates. Someone in the balcony said "shhhh" and the whole theater stopped to watch the usher. The usher walked over to our seats and offered the roses and chocolates to my partner and announced that they were compliments of me. You could hear the sighs from all of the wives or girlfriends within fifty feet. You could also see the frowns and looks of intimidation on the faces of their husbands and boyfriends. I am sure there were a lot of sore ribs that evening. Who became preferred? With just a little up-level personal attention, I became the preferred companion at the theater that night!

Remember to take whatever you are doing for someone and up-level it as much as you can. Think of this as a creative adventure! You will have fun doing it, your clients will have fun receiving it, and best of all they will remember you and talk about you to their friends. This will generate huge networking rewards. To make it work in your business situation, identify the services that you are currently offering and ask yourself what you would have to do to make your customers say "wow"! Remember that High Touch should have little to do with your company, your products, or your services. Rather it should be the discretionary effort that you make towards your clients and customers (or your personal relationships) that exceeds their expectations and creates an extraordinary experience. Doing this makes an ordinary experience become an emotional one. And, as you may recall, our customers buy first for emotional reasons and then justify their purchases with logic.

The Relationship Bank

The reason why the High Touch strategy is so effective is because of the value/price relationship. This dictates that when you bring little value to the relationship, the price of doing business with you is a big deal. If there is not enough perceived value in what you offer, then the inconvenience of changing to you is too great and your potential customers will likely not do it. On the other hand, if you deliver high value as your potential customers define it, then the value and perceived value

"We must bring value
to the marketplace as
the marketplace defines
value – not as we do!"

will be there and the inconvenience associated with the change to your products or services will be significantly diminished.

Value / Price Relationship

$$\text{Value} = \text{Price}$$

$$\text{Value} = \text{Price}$$

I work hard to maintain a healthy balance in my business accounts. I also focus on maintaining a healthy balance in my relationship accounts. Business relationships–in fact any relationships–grow stronger through regular deposits. If I am running a deficit in my relationship accounts, I am on my way out whether I know it or not. I never want my clients doing more for me (i.e., treating me as a preferred supplier and giving me their business) than I am doing for them (i.e., treating them as a preferred client and bringing value as they define it).

Here is a story that illustrates this balance. Let us suppose that you are at a point in your life where you want to get married. When you first find that person you think you might want to have a long-term relationship with, you probably do not have enough deposits in the relationship bank account for them to say "yes" to any kind of long-term commitment. So, for example, if you asked your new relationship partner to marry you after only a few dates you could probably predict that the outcome would be negative. Over time, however, if you made enough deposits into the relationship bank account, you might get a "yes" to a long-term commitment. How do you make significant deposits into the relationship bank account? Learn about your partner's value system. What does he or she care about? What is the best currency to use when making deposits into this relationship account? The sooner you learn what is valuable to them, the sooner you are able to create value for them and contribute to them in a way that will make your relationship stronger.

Take the time, however, to carefully understand the needs of your partner, whether it is a personal or business relationship. Failure to do so can have the opposite effect than the one you intend. From a relationship standpoint, this means that you can potentially damage the relationship rather than contribute to it. Here is an example from my own experience where wrong assumptions probably damaged rather than contributed to a relationship.

I wanted to do something really special for my significant other on one of our anniversaries, and I knew that she needed a new watch. So I went out and put a deposit down on a very expensive watch, a Rolex, something that she would be proud of for years to come. The big occasion was fast approaching, and I was getting really excited. I was like a kid on Christmas Eve. I could not wait to give her the present. The big day finally arrived and I said somewhat jokingly, "Honey, Happy Anniversary, Happy Birthday and Merry Christmas for the next ten years." She responded with, "Wow, what did you get?" I handed her the carefully wrapped package. She pulled the wrapping off the case, exposing the Rolex logo and she exclaimed, "It's a Rolex!" "Why, yes it is," I said proudly. She looked at me and said, "But I hate Rolex watches."

"Excuse me! I could have sworn you said you hate Rolex watches, how funny is that. What did you say?" She repeated her original statement. I was shocked. "I thought you said you wanted a new watch." "I do," she responded, "but I want one of those Timex watches –you know, the kind with the second-hand stopwatch so that I can time eggs." (Long pause) She then looked at me and said: "Mike, you look disappointed." "Duh!" I responded. Then she asked me a question that went right to the heart of the matter. "Mike, did you buy the watch for me or did you buy it for you?" Ouch! Good question. She handed the case back to me and told me to take it back. I took it back (and now I have a really cool motorcycle). You would think that I would have known my number one relationship better than that. But I assumed wrong.

Let me give you another example of the importance of understanding the needs of your relationship partners. I was walking past a pottery store. What caught my attention was a woman sitting at the window at a pottery wheel. You could hear beautiful music and there she was sitting there with wet clay streaming through her fingers. It reminded me of the famous scene at the pottery wheel in the movie *Ghost*. I went into the store and the lady at the window, who was probably about seventy years old, helped me make a serving platter and dipping bowl for my significant other. I painted my creation with three coats of paint, lots of different designs, and then had it fired in the kiln. I spent $38 in parts and the better part of the day making it. But it was unique, it was creative, and I just knew it was the kind of thing my partner would love. I was right. This gift was an unbelievable hit. She cried! And I earned massive relationship points.

Just as our personal relationships have an implied point system, our client relationships do as well. You cannot assume what that point system is, for assumptions can get you into trouble. Rather, to be certain of what they find valuable you must ask them, and most importantly, you must listen carefully to their responses. Odds are it will have nothing whatsoever to do with your core competencies or High Task functionality. You might be in for quite a surprise when you start asking these types of questions of your clients and potential clients and even of your personal relationship partners.

The most powerful relationship on earth is arguably the marital relationship. It forms, and has formed, the core of our societal norms for thousands of years. But consider many typical marriages today. It almost seems like you put the ring on the finger and it is immediately like pulling a rip-cord to an inflatable raft. The pot belly appears as quickly as the pre-marital exercise routines seem to disappear. Out come all of the nasty habits. Maybe he is leaving his dirty socks and odors all over the house. Maybe she quits doing all of the things that he loved and found valuable when they were courting. The reality is, that according to recent statistics, in 56 percent of the cases, the marriage will end in divorce. More than half of the time, the most powerful strategic alliance on the planet blows apart. Does this mean that the other 44 percent of us are happily elated with the deal that we made? Not quite. Many more stay together out of economic convenience, or because of children, or because there is not another "supplier" currently out there vying for their business!

"To truly insulate
our clients from
competitive erosion,
we must discover
what they value."

If this is true of our personal relationships, what does it say about our business relationships? How many of your customers are staying with you only because it is too much of an inconvenience to change, or there is not another vendor or supplier available–yet? Personal relationships end a majority of the time because we tend to take them for granted. Do you suppose that we might take our business or economic relationships for granted as well?

The bottom line is that our clients have a point system that is different from our own. They keep score differently than we do. Often what we think is high value, they think is low value. To truly insulate our clients from competitive erosion, we must discover what they value. We must understand their point system and treat them in the way they prefer to be treated. Even within the same industry, all clients are not alike. When I ask my audiences how many of them have clients that only want to do business with them, a sea of enthusiastic hands always go into the air. It is a great feeling to bring lots of value to customers. And it breeds confidence in business when you understand the customer's point system and you can contribute to their relationship account because you understand it. Nothing is better than having clients do business with you because they highly value and appreciate what you bring to the table.

New Client Attraction

Now let us take this a little further. Let us move from enhancing our current relationships to attracting new ones. For example, have you ever made a sales call only to be told that the prospect is currently using your competitor and is quite happy with their services? In short, they are not interested in hearing what you have to say. This prospect is not rejecting you personally, because they do not know you personally (once they get to know you, then they can reject you). The reason they feel comfortable in sending you packing is this: You have not yet demonstrated to them value as they define it. Therefore, they do not know what they are missing, and they can say goodbye to you with a clear conscience.

When the value you bring to the table is small, the price of doing business with you is big. The pain of changing from an existing relationship is too great compared to any perceived benefits you might be able to show. And yet there might still be an opportunity. The key lies not in the products or services that you offer relative to your competitors, but in the potential value that a relationship with you can bring to them. Lots of your competitors are out there taking their key relationships for granted. Their account balances will certainly be low. To win the business of their clients, you simply need to have a chance to show them the value that you can bring.

I have a tactic that is a real winner when it comes to creating such a chance and ultimately taking business away from competitors. It is called the "Second Place Strategy." Let us assume that you are visiting an account, you ask for their business, and you hear something like this: "Sorry, we have been using your competitor now for about five years, and we are quite happy with the service they are providing." This is your opportunity to use the Second Place Strategy. You respond, "Well, Mr. Prospect, I certainly appreciate the value of long-term relationships. Our company also strives to maintain such relationships with our clients. With your permission, I would like to position myself and my company to be your number two vendor. Here is what that means. I don't need a contract or a check, I just need your verbal okay to have access to you from time to time, to bring you information that might be of value to you. In the event that the first place vendor does not measure up or cannot deliver on any business request that you might have, then I would like a chance to step up to bat. I think you will agree that it makes good business sense to have a back-up option in hand. May I have second place?"

"Sure," says Mr. Prospect, "now go away." So you leave, you go back to your office, and you send out a thank you note that reads something like this: "Dear Mr. Prospect, thank you for giving me second place. I will work hard to earn your trust. Regards, Michael." Three weeks later you send him five tips on how to improve

"To be successful in retaining and attracting clients, we must appreciate them, and we must demonstrate that appreciation by providing value."

office productivity, with another note: "I thought this might be of value to you. Regards, Michael." Every month for the next three or four months, you send him some knowledge-based Distinctive Value. Something he will value and that will help him resolve an issue you know he is facing. The important point to remember is that it should not have anything to do with the product or service you are offering.

Do you think the first place vendor is doing this? Maybe, but it is unlikely. By asking for second place you have earned the right to compete against the first place vendor. Now you simply have to do a better job than the first place vendor. Avis made a billion dollar business out of this. Remember their slogan: "We're number two....we try harder." We are all guilty of taking relationships for granted. We do it all of the time. The simple truth about human nature is that we are not appreciative enough, nor are we usually very good at demonstrating our appreciation. It is easy for us to take things for granted. But just as it takes a lot of work to create a healthy personal relationship, it also takes a lot of work to create a healthy economic or business relationship. To be successful in retaining and attracting clients, we must appreciate them, and we must demonstrate that appreciation by providing value. The Second Place Strategy is an effective way of creating the opportunity to create this pleasure or value for your prospective clients.

Let us take a look at what we have covered so far. We have learned that our initial focus should be on identifying the needs of our clients so we can address these needs better than our competitors. Because our customers buy first emotionally, then justify their purchase with logic, we are going to sell the way they like to buy. That means we are going to provide our core competencies and our high task stuff, but we are going to balance it with a high touch customer service strategy–that is we are going to exceed our clients' or prospects' expectations of the relationship.

We exceed our clients' expectations by bringing value to the marketplace as our market defines it. In the event that we cannot get the first position with a prospective client, we will use the second place strategy, and hopefully earn the right to compete for first place. With that opportunity, we will make regular deposits into the relationship bank account by dripping knowledge-based Distinctive Value to our clients and prospective clients. We will demonstrate to them that we can provide a stronger and more valued service than their primary vendor.

Personality Dynamics

The subject of relationship building would not be complete if I did not remind you of something quite important. As you develop relationships within your market, you must remember the variation of personalities that exist, and you must do everything possible to communicate with each of your clients or prospective clients in a manner that matches their personality or communication style. You might have had some training in personality or communication styles already, using the Myers-Briggs Type Indicator or other human resources tools to gain insight into the buyer. There has been a lot said on personality and buying styles over the years, and there have been many different approaches to understanding personality styles. All of them are useful in better understanding human personalities and all of them work to one degree or another. I have digested much of this available information, and from it have created my own hybrid version that I believe best describes the marketplace in which most of us work.

Here are four titles that are easy to remember and that generally describe the personality styles of most of your clients and prospects:

Expressives
Directors
Analyticals
Amiables

Each of these four styles of personalities has their own unique way of making purchasing decisions. You maximize your chance of successfully working with someone when you understand their personality style. Let us take a closer look at each of the styles.

Expressives

The first of the four personality styles is the Expressive. The buying patterns of Expressives are largely driven by image. The majority of their decisions are made on the basis of how the outcome will make them look, even though this is not always their conscious intention. Expressive personalities are usually well dressed, wear the latest fashions, and, quite often set the trends within their organizations. They are not adverse to taking risks, providing there is a potential payoff. If you were to walk into their office, you would most likely find pictures of themselves with celebrities as well as their trophies and awards. They are very open in their approach; they laugh, they have fun, and they are eternal optimists. The glass is always half full for an Expressive. Their primary concern is how a choice will affect them or benefit them, especially in the eyes of others. Expressives do not like to get bogged down with details, and they are most happy when dealing with the big picture.

If you were listening to an Expressive client or prospect you would hear questions like:

Will it benefit us?

Is it the best?

Can I help?

Is it fair?

Here is how I suggest that you interact with an Expressive:

Be enthusiastic and friendly.

Establish rapport before making proposals.

Ask personal questions.

Wine, dine, and entertain them.

Reduce the paperwork load for them.

Ask them for their opinion.

Use personal stories and experiences in your presentations.

Emphasize how it will positively affect their status.

Be sociable and outgoing.

Keep the conversation moving.

Recognize their classy apparel.

Recognize their position or title.

Emphasize the popular benefits of products and services.

Here are some phrases that motivate Expressives:

This is a brand new or leading edge technology.

This will give you a competitive advantage in the marketplace.

This is new to the market.

This will help you build market prestige or dominance.

It enables you greater access to well known people.

It will boost your image.

It will improve your social life.

It is an innovative idea.

This is going to be a lot of fun!

Here are a few of our key clients.

The major drivers in the personal buying style of Expressives are as follows:

They like recognition or publicity.

They like the first, the biggest, and the best.

They want things that are innovative and unique.

Expressives are likely to buy when a project or proposal:

Has creative ideas.

Has good references.

Sounds good and feels good.

Are you starting to get the picture? When they make their buying decisions, a number of factors will go into the process. They will want to know whether the solution is innovative or unique. They will want to know (but might not ask) how it will make them appear to their colleagues and peers. And they will want to know whether the solution you are offering is the best one available.

Expressives love big deals and new and creative ideas. As long as the references check out and the deal feels good, they are likely to go for it if it appears unique. When you communicate with an Expressive, make your time with them entertaining, stimulating, fun, and fast moving. Make sure you leave time for socializing, offering special deals, extras, or incentives, and do not forget to ask for their opinions and ideas.

Directors

The second of the four personality styles is the Directors. These are the people that are oriented to the bottom-line. They are so direct that they almost appear to be rude. They are not at all interested in

pleasantries; they just want to get down to business.
They are usually conservative in nature and in dress. If
you were to walk into their office it would look
organized and practical. They tend to be a little closed
and keep their cards close to the vest. They care little
about anything other than the results. If you are
presenting to a director-type personality, make sure
that you leave out all the fluff and get to the bottom-
line quickly. They will appreciate it.

If you were listening to a Director client or prospect you would hear questions like:

What are the opportunities?

What is the bottom-line?

Who is in control?

What is next?

What is the result?

Here is how I suggest that you interact with a Director:

Be prepared and be organized.

Do not waste their time.

Let them make the final decision.

Be on time, or better yet, be early.

Follow up in a timely manner.

Do not be too sociable.

Be concise and to the point.

Handle their problems and concerns professionally.

Point out how they profit financially.

Present proposals backed up with research.

Do not give unnecessary details unless asked for.

Do not waste their time with idle chit-chat.

Pay attention to the details.

Always set up your briefing in advance.

Gain an understanding of their business.

Here are some phrases that motivate Directors:

This is the bottom-line.

I will be brief and to the point.

This is how you will benefit financially.

Here is an executive summary that I have prepared for you.

This will save you time.

Here are a couple of options to work with.

When do you want us to start?

I know your time is valuable.

Here are several solutions to work with.

What works best for you?

When is the most convenient time to see you?

This will allow you to stay very focused.

This is how your organization will benefit financially.

Here is the bottom-line cost.

Can you see the difference between Expressives and Directors? All of the flattery and attention that you would spend on an Expressive won't go very far with a Director. Better to keep you and them focused on results and the bottom-line.

The major drivers in the personal buying style of Directors are as follows:

They want more personal power.

They want increased control.

They like choices and options.

Directors are likely to buy when a project or proposal:

Will get bottom-line results.

Gets the job done.

Will be on schedule and under budget.

When you communicate with a Director, remember to be brief, specific, and to the point. Stick to business and do not chit-chat with them. Come prepared with all the necessary information, objectives, and support materials in a well-organized package. Plan to present the facts cleanly and logically. Provide alternative solutions and let them make the decision. After talking business, leave right away–do not hang around too long or you will quickly outstay your welcome.

Analyticals

The third personality style is the Analyticals. These people are consumed with facts, figures, specifications, and logistics. They thrive on the details. They want loads of information to help them with their analysis. Analyticals have a need to be right and usually are–that is why they require large amounts of data. Because they tend to research everything, they are often slow to make a decision. Within an organization, Analyticals are usually not the ones making decisions, but they do support them, especially when grounded in evidence. If you were to walk into the office of an Analytical you would probably see papers everywhere. It might look like a mess, but don't touch a thing; they know exactly where everything is.

If you were listening to an Analytical client or prospect, you would hear questions like:

What are the trade-offs?

How does it work?

Who does what?

Can we sample?

What support do you have for that observation?

Here is how I suggest that you interact with an Analytical:

Be organized.

Be prepared with statistics.

Provide detailed data on paper.

Do not be too sociable or too chatty.

Emphasize value and reliability.

Let them think things over when making a decision.

Do not be vague and unprepared–be an expert.

Provide technical details and ask technical questions.

Be professional.

Be logical in your presentation.

Get to the point quickly.

Avoid emotional questions.

Do not make up answers.

Provide factual research to answer their questions.

Emphasize value and reliability.

Make them aware of possible outcomes.

Provide handouts for them to keep.

Here are some phrases that motivate Analyticals:

Here are the pros and cons.

Let me show you all the details.

Here are possible problems and their solutions.

Take your time to make a decision.

Based upon your expertise, how would you design a project?

Here are a number of technical papers we have written on the subject.

I will research it for you.

It is reliable based upon the following statistics.

Can I make an appointment to see you?

Based upon the product's past track record, there have never been any surprises.

Would you like to see our quality control processes?

It comes with detailed instructions.

The major drivers in the personal buying style of Analyticals are as follows:

They want to be respected as an expert.

They take pride in staff work.

They have a need to be right.

Analyticals are likely to buy when a project or proposal:

Meets specifications.

Meets goals and objectives.

Is the most logical solution.

When you communicate with an Analytical, be as accurate as you can. Be direct and stick to business. List pros and cons to any suggestions you make. Take your time, but be persistent. Provide tangible practical evidence and provide guarantees over a long period of time. But perhaps most importantly, give options.

Amiables

The last of the four personality styles is the Amiables. Amiables are really easy to get along with, are very friendly, and do not like confrontation. If you were to visit the office of an Amiable you would find pictures of their families, children and pets. Amiables are not risk takers; they want to be sure of their decisions. Therefore, they want lots of case studies. Their approach to life is to do something because "everybody is doing it." They are not the first person to buy the latest and greatest thing. That is the job of the Expressive. Amiables want to make sure that everything is tried and proven so they can feel secure in their decisions.

If you were listening to an Amiable client or prospect you would hear questions like:

What are people's opinions?

Will it gain acceptance?

Can it be changed?

Is it disruptive?

Here is how I suggest that you interact with an Amiable:

Be friendly and sociable.

Use referrals.

Be polite and likeable.

Be sensitive.

Ask for their opinion.

Point out guarantees.

Let them take time to consult others when making decisions.

Recognize birthdays and holidays.

Drop by casually.

Be their consultant.

Here are some phrases that motivate Amiables:

Let's solve this problem together.

Can I give you my opinion?

How do you feel about it?

This has a guarantee with it.

How is your family doing?

Here is a list of our most loyal clients.

Everyone is doing it.

This product will not rock the boat.

I believe your colleagues will be pleased with your decision.

The major drivers in the personal buying style of Amaibles are as follows:

Like, trust, and respect.

They want to see group consensus.

They like to avoid conflict or controversy.

Amiables are likely to buy when a project or proposal:

Meets with staff or committee approval.

Has guarantees or assurances.

Has tried and proven solutions.

When you communicate with an Amiable, start with a personal comment to break the ice. Show sincere interest in them as people, find areas of common involvement, and be candid with them. Be sure to listen, and be responsive to their requests for information. Be non-threatening, casual, and informal. Provide assurances and guarantees that their decision will minimize risk and harm to others.

Customization

Perhaps you have noticed that you have a little of each of the personality types. That is because the styles are generalities, and no one person fits cleanly into any of them. As a result, there is a subgroup in each style. So it is possible, for instance, to be an Expressive/Director, or a Director/Director. The bottom line, however, is that it does not matter what style you are. This is an exercise to better understand the personality needs of your clients and prospects. Consequently, use this information to understand your clients and communicate with them in the manner that they communicate.

In today's competitive global marketplace, it is more important than ever that you present your products and services in their most favorable light. That means not only understanding the personalities of the people with whom you interact, but also understanding the style of company that you are dealing with, and their cultural background. For example, one of my clients is from Finland. Their culture is dramatically different than companies from North America. They are very analytical in their decision-making process. However, relative to North American firms, they appear very Expressive in their style. I have had to create a hybrid approach when dealing with this company, taking into consideration both their Expressive and their Analytical natures.

Your proposals should be customized to your audience. Often we write proposals based on our style, and thus we only win a certain part of the business. Technically speaking, you should have at least four different proposals that consider each of the buying styles. If you take into consideration all of the sub-categories, you could extend that number considerably. However, the bottom line remains the same: Remember to sell to people in the way that they want to buy.

CONCLUSION

Let us wrap things up. This book has focused on three strategies that, if applied, will give you a competitive advantage. They are so powerful that even the successful execution of any of them individually can do the trick. Remember that in section one we focused on creating Distinctive Value. This is a great strategy for becoming preferred because in essence you create your own markets. If you are successful, your competitors will create a "me too," and you will find downward pressures on your margins. The lesson is simple. What is distinctive today becomes just value tomorrow. Eat your own lunch before your competition does. Innovate or perish.

The sales process in section two is important because it teaches you how to define your markets, gain access

"What is distinctive today becomes just value tomorrow. Eat your own lunch before your competition does. Innovate or perish."

to the decision-makers, and position yourself in the mind of the prospect. Let me suggest that even if your product or service is not distinctive, you can still win the business with a well executed sales process. Take a good look at your own process and innovate it. Make sure that it is flexible and that you have your action steps outlined not just when they say "yes" and you make the sell, but also when they say "no". Remember, the harder they are to get, the better they are when you get them.

Last but not least we have the business relationship. Again, assuming you do not have Distinctive Value, assuming you do not have a sales process, you can still win and keep the business if your relationship is better. The relationship trumps all of the strategies. It trumps them because people buy first emotionally and then justify the purchase logically. The fact is that if they like you more than your competitors you win.

Imagine if you applied all three strategies to your business model. The fact is you would kick some serious butt in the marketplace. It is up to you to decide. You can either let these strategies go in one ear and out the other or you can apply and execute them. This part is up to you. I can tell you from my experience that they work; they work because they make sense. My clients from all over North America let me know this on a regular basis. I get letters and emails from sales professionals who were stalled in their careers thanking me for reinvigorating their careers. I get letters from entrepreneurs, leaders of organizations, and company presidents thanking me for contributing to their success. My clients have transformed their organizations and processes to better position themselves to do business in the new millennium. If you apply what has been presented in this book, you will add value to yourself, your organization, and your company. You will move up the income ladder significantly, and you will move from job or market security to self security.

And you will become preferred.